saltysweets

salty sweets

DELECTABLE DESSERTS
AND TEMPTING TREATS WITH
A SUBLIME KISS OF SALT

christie matheson

PHOTOGRAPHS BY JOYCE OUDKERK POOL

THE HARVARD COMMON PRESS
BOSTON, MASSACHUSETTS

The Harvard Common Press
535 Albany Street
Boston, Massachusetts 02118
www.harvardcommonpress.com

Printed in China
Printed on acid-free paper

Library of Congress Cataloging-in-Publication Data
Matheson, Christie.
  Salty sweets : delectable desserts and tempting treats with a sublime kiss of salt / Christie Matheson.
    p. cm.
  Includes index.
  ISBN 978-1-55832-415-2
  1. Desserts. I. Title.
  TX773.M294 2009
  641.8'6--dc22
                                        2008055567
Paper-over-board edition: ISBN 978-1-55832-556-2

Special bulk-order discounts are available on this and other Harvard Common Press books. Companies and organizations may purchase books for premiums or resale, or may arrange a custom edition, by contacting the Marketing Director at the address above.

Book design by Elizabeth Van Itallie
Photography by Joyce Oudkerk Pool
Food styling by Jen Straus
Props by Tabletop Prop

10 9 8 7 6 5 4 3 2 1

To my mom, Pat Matheson, who always encouraged me to play in the kitchen

contents

acknowledgments

Thanks to my agent, Stacey Glick, who is endlessly supportive and thoughtful—and who shares my specific fondness for peanut buttery salty sweets. I'm lucky to know you. Thanks to The Harvard Common Press for understanding the vital importance of a book about salty sweets. Working with the team at HCP—Valerie Cimino, Jane Dornbusch, Virginia Downes, Janice Geary, Pat Jalbert-Levine, Vicki Rowland, Howard Stelzer, and Betsy Young—is truly a pleasure. Thank you all for taking such good care of me! Thanks to Joyce Oudkerk Pool for the pretty pictures, and to Jen Straus for lovely, unfussy food styling. Thanks to the pastry chefs who inspire me with their creativity and imagination, especially Joanne Chang, Gale Gand, and Elisa Strauss. Thanks to everyone who taste-tested recipes—it's not always easy to give honest feedback, and I appreciate it greatly. (Quick shout-out to first-time guinea pig Sydney James, who took a bite of an ice cream test, made a face, and told me she didn't like it at all.) Thanks to my brother, Seth Matheson, for sharing ideas about food and dreaming up wacky combinations. Most of all, thanks to Will Adams, who is willing to try anything I make and who makes every day so sweet.

In gratitude to organizations working to end hunger locally and around the world, I am donating a portion of the proceeds from *Salty Sweets* to the Greater Boston Food Bank (gbfb.org), the San Francisco Food Bank (sffoodbank.org), and the United Nations World Food Programme (wfp.org).

prelude to a kiss (of salt)

My favorite sweets are the ones that excite the palate and stimulate a whole bunch of taste buds. What's the point of indulging in a sweet treat if it's not going to knock your socks off? Disappointing desserts are so . . . disappointing. I don't want to have to eat a whole plate of cookies or a ginormous piece of cake to feel satisfied. I like sweets that are so darn good that a little goes a long way—as long as I can resist the temptation to sneak an extra bite. That kind of temptation, mind you, is quite different from one that leads you mindlessly and repeatedly to eat spoonfuls of flavorless ice cream from the carton or handfuls of bland cookies that aren't really doing it for you. (Um, not that I've ever done that.)

A few years ago I realized that the most satisfying and rewarding sweets are the ones that have something going on other than straight-up sweetness. Sweet is sweet, but it can be kind of one-dimensional. But when you add a *salty* element to said sweet—even if the result is not an overtly salty flavor—the treat in question gets seriously amped up.

I'm not the only one who thinks so. Salty-sweet desserts are showing up more and more often on menus at outstanding restaurants all over the country. When friends rave about a caramel they just tried or gush about a new ice cream flavor, it almost always has some kind of salty component. At one of the trendy gourmet cupcake shops in San Francisco, when *fleur de sel* chocolate cupcakes are that day's special, they always sell out. Grownups love salty sweets, and so do kids (hello, PB & J sandwiches)—and they will devour the Chocolate Chip Cookies that you'll find on page 44.

Of course, salt has always been an important part of baking. Many recipes use it as a leavening agent, and the recipes in this book do, too. But salt is also important to the flavor of a dessert, beyond its pure chemical function. Making salty sweets isn't about dumping a little extra salt into every dessert you make, though. If something is too salty, it won't taste good.

When I was growing up, I loved to experiment in the kitchen, and I was very lucky to have a mom who let me do that. One day when I was about eight years old, I wanted to make chocolate chip cookies. I read the recipe and told my mom I didn't think cookies needed any salt. She tried to explain, but

I didn't want to listen. "Okay," she said. "Try them without salt and see what you think." Not so good.

Salt, when used judiciously, heightens the flavors of foods and stimulates the palate—sometimes sending it into ecstatic excitement when combined with the right other ingredients. It brings out the complexities of chocolate, highlights the subtleties of fruit, and makes the flavor of nuts pop. It transforms traditional sweet flavors like caramel and butterscotch into something truly special. To me, there's nothing as mouthwatering and delicious as a good salty sweet.

Salty sweets don't have to be complicated to taste good. Most of the recipes in this book are pretty simple, in fact. They can even be as simple as a recipe that my husband, Will, came up with when he was in second grade. Will's mother, Lee, gave it to me when we got engaged—it's written in very careful handwriting on lined school paper (the teacher graded him with a smiley face), and I love it. Here's what he wrote: "Make some peanut butter candy. You need 1 cup peanut butter, 1 cup corn syrup, 1¼ cups powdered milk, 1¼ cups powdered sugar. First mix it. Roll it into little balls. Then ea it." (He forgot the "t" in eat.) The peanut butter is the salty-sweet element, and you might add ¼ teaspoon of fine sea salt, too. There you have it—a simple salty sweet. I hope you enjoy it—and the other recipes in this book, too.

A FEW RANDOM THOUGHTS ON MAKING SWEETS

Though I've spent countless hours in restaurant and bakery kitchens working with chefs on their cookbooks, I am first and foremost a home cook and baker. But I've learned a lot from watching chefs in action. The key thing that they all seem to do: Hire a staff of eager young cooks and dishwashers. If you do that, your baking life will quickly get easier. No? Your kitchen staff isn't arriving anytime soon? Mine isn't either. So keep a few of these concepts in mind.

Mise en place! This translates from the French to "set in place," and it means getting all your ducks in a row before you begin a recipe (or at least getting all your ingredients in a row). It's the reason Food Network chefs always look like they're breezing through the kitchen effortlessly: Everything is ready already. Ingredients are measured, mixer attachments are located, and bowls are cleaned and dried. Taking time to get set up before you start a recipe makes life so much easier, and it saves you time and frustration throughout the process. This is especially important in baking, because precise measurements matter and timing is often crucial.

Use the best ingredients. This is a universal truth of cooking and baking: The better the ingredients, the better the final product. It's especially true when you're making simple dishes—like most of the recipes in this book—in which the flavors of a few key ingredients are the stars of the show. Look for quality ingredients, and opt for organic whenever you can. Not only is the production of organic ingredients (such as fruits, chocolate, milk, and eggs) better for the planet, these ingredients taste better and are better for you, too.

Always choose organic chocolate. Conventional chocolate is often grown on plantations where rainforests have been clear-cut to allow full sun to reach the cacao plants. But cacao grows best—and doesn't need synthetic fertilizers and pesticides—under the shade of a rainforest canopy. Buying organic chocolate means keeping potentially harmful chemicals out of your body and helping to save the rainforest. Thank you, in advance.

Buy local honey and support local beekeepers whenever you can. The bee population in the United States has been dwindling in recent years, and no one quite knows why. But experts do know that bees are hugely important if we want them to keep pollinating fruit trees—and they also believe that small, local beekeepers may be helping to preserve the bee population. So buy your honey locally! The same is true for fruits: Choose fruits in season, and support local organic farmers whenever you can. Locally grown fruits taste delicious and are richer in nutrients than produce that's been shipped thousands of miles or that's been sitting around in a warehouse, and buying local and organic is a great choice for the planet.

Be patient. Taking shortcuts while cooking isn't always the best idea, and spending a little extra time to do things right can greatly improve the results (and, of course, it often saves you time in the end). Following are a few techniques—none of them difficult—for which doing it right is preferable to doing it fast.

techniques

▪ MELTING CHOCOLATE. When a recipe calls for melted chocolate, avoid melting the chocolate in a pan over direct heat. The chocolate could easily scorch if you do it that way. Instead, chop the chocolate and place it in a heatproof glass or metal bowl, then place the bowl over—not in—a pan of simmering water (or use a double boiler) and let it heat gently, stirring occasionally to encourage even melting. Do not cover the chocolate during or after melting, because you don't want any condensation to drip into the chocolate (water and melted chocolate don't mix—the chocolate could seize, or harden). When you remove the bowl from over the simmering water, do so using a kitchen towel, which serves double duty as a potholder and to wipe the bottom of the bowl free of moisture. If you are pouring the chocolate, don't let any condensation from the outside of the bowl get into the chocolate.

▪ TOASTING NUTS. When a recipe calls for toasted nuts, take the time to toast them. Toasting brings out the flavor of the nut and makes it more intense, meaning your recipe will taste better. It doesn't take long. Heat the oven to 350°F and spread the nuts evenly on a baking sheet. Toast for 7 to 10 minutes, until golden brown and just fragrant. Be careful not to let them get too dark or burn, because then they will taste bitter. Remove them from the oven and let them cool before using in most recipes.

▪ TEMPERING EGGS. If you dump a lot of hot liquid into raw eggs all at once, you will cook the eggs and wind up with something that looks more like breakfast (scrambled eggs) than dessert. When a recipe calls for adding hot liquid to eggs in small increments, do it slowly, as directed.

▪ MEASURING FLOUR. If you're in a rush, it's tempting to stick your measuring scoop into a bag of flour and get your entire ½ cup or 1 cup at once, but that will give you too much flour, and your pastries could end up denser and drier than you want. To measure flour properly, lightly and gently scoop it in spoonfuls into your measuring cup. Don't pack it in, and use a straight edge, like the back of a knife, to level the surface and fill the cup to the rim.

■ SIFTING FLOUR. Cake recipes often call for sifting flour, and when they do, it's worth the time. It doesn't take long, and it will help give your cake a lighter and fluffier texture.

For every recipe, give yourself time! All these techniques that require patience remind me that it's a good idea to allow plenty of time to complete a recipe and let it cool or freeze, if necessary. Baking great treats should be fun, not stressful, and all the recipes in this book are totally doable, but making anything is a much lovelier experience when you don't feel pressed for time. Relax, read the entire recipe before you start, turn on some music, get your ingredients and equipment ready, and enjoy!

equipment

You don't need to have a kitchen stocked with every last culinary toy in order to enjoy baking. In fact, if all you have is a mixing bowl, a wooden spoon, and a few baking pans, you can probably make most of these recipes. But here are a few gizmos I strongly recommend.

■ STAND MIXER. A good stand mixer makes the life of a baker ever so much easier. It doesn't have to be an over-the-top, restaurant-style setup with hundreds of bells and whistles. A basic stand mixer will do a lot of the work of creaming, whipping, stirring, and blending for you in no time.

■ ICE CREAM MAKER. This just might be my favorite kitchen toy. It is so much fun to make your own ice cream and then to experiment with flavor combinations once you have the hang of a few basic recipes. And it's easy to use! An ice cream maker doesn't have to be pricey, either. You can pick up a good-quality Cuisinart ice cream maker for about $50 or an ice cream maker attachment for a KitchenAid stand mixer for around $80.

■ CANDY THERMOMETER. You can get by without one of these, as I did for years, but that might make you afraid—and reasonably so—to try any recipe that mentions one. Making things like caramel and fudge without one can be tricky, because sugar behaves in very specific ways at different temperatures, and trying to guess whether a bubbling pot of goo is 230° or 250°F is impossible. With a candy thermometer, there's almost no guesswork. They aren't expensive (mine was less than $20), and they are simple to use.

■ SIFTER. Become friends with your sifter. Yes, it takes an extra minute or two to sift flour and other dry ingredients, but it makes a nice difference in the texture of your cakes and cupcakes.

■ ICE CREAM SCOOP. Handy for doling out equal-size portions of cookie dough and for filling muffin tins, this is also the ideal tool for—you guessed it—scooping ice cream.

■ SALT GRINDER. You can purchase finely ground and coarsely ground sea salt, but when you want salt with a little more texture than fine, but not quite the heft of coarse, a grinder does the trick. I keep mine loaded with coarse sea salt and I use it to grind (and distribute evenly and easily) salt lightly over cookies and cakes. Many salt grinders have an adjustable grinding mechanism so that you can regulate the coarseness to suit your textural preferences. It might seem like more of an investment to buy a salt grinder and bulk salts than to purchase those pre-filled, disposable salt grinders you see in the spice section at most grocery stores, but you can refill a grinder with the salt of your choice, and over time it will be a money-saver. (Plus it's more earth-friendly to use—less packaging.) Look for a good-quality grinder with a ceramic grinding mechanism, which won't be corroded by the salt.

salt primer (everything you always wanted to know about salt but were afraid to ask)

All salt is not created equal. The iodized table salt that many of us grew up with is salty, sure, but it has been refined and stripped of minerals and treated with anti-caking agents. And it just doesn't have very good salt flavor. Kosher salt is preferable to table salt; it is coarser and has no added iodine, so the flavor is more pure. If that's what you have on hand, you can substitute kosher salt for sea salt. For flavor, though, I think sea salt is the way to go, and that is what I call for in these recipes. It's harvested from seawater, and it tastes the way salt is meant to taste.

There are many, many varieties of sea salt. Most of the recipes in this book call for either fine sea salt, coarse sea salt, grinder sea salt, or *fleur de sel*. Here's some more information on each kind:

■ FINE SEA SALT. This is a great all-purpose sea salt that I use for many recipes. It dissolves readily and has delicious flavor.

■ COARSE SEA SALT. This sea salt has a much larger grain than fine sea salt. It doesn't dissolve as well, so it's not a good substitute for the chemically required salt in many baking recipes, but it adds lovely salt flavor and interesting texture to recipes.

■ GRINDER SEA SALT. This is coarse salt that you grind yourself right when you need it—it comes out medium-ground, coarser than a fine grain but not in big crystals.

■ *FLEUR DE SEL.* French for "flower of salt," it's the slightly sweeter white layer of salt generally harvested by hand from salt ponds in France. *C'est magnifique!*

In this book, I didn't want to call for a different kind of specialty salt in every single recipe, but I do encourage you to experiment with a variety of salts. Different salts really do have distinct tastes, so buy small amounts and discover what flavor combinations you like. Especially in the recipes that call for *fleur de sel*, consider trying another artisan sea salt, such as one of the following:

■ *SEL GRIS.* An unrefined gray salt found off the coast of France, *sel gris* is generally coarse, fairly moist, and rich in minerals.

■ MALDON SALT. A light, flaky, flavorful white sea salt from the British coast, Maldon is a favorite finishing salt (a salt added to a dish—sweet or savory—just before serving) of many chefs and foodies I know.

■ SMOKED SEA SALT. Infused with a deep, smoky flavor—subtly different depending on what kind of wood is used to smoke it—smoked sea salt is usually dark in color and adds a surprisingly earthy kick to recipes.

■ TROPICAL SEA SALT. Rich in minerals, tropical sea salt is harvested from oceans in warm climates, and tends to have a mellow yet decidedly sea-like flavor. My brother-in-law David and his partner, Cory, gave me a Bali sea salt that I particularly love to use as a finishing salt for fruity sweets.

■ HAWAIIAN PINK SEA SALT. Enriched with iron oxide from volcanic red clay, Hawaiian sea salt is subtle and distinctive in flavor—try it with spicy island foods and play around with it to see what other combinations work for you.

There are countless other salts to sample, from Maine sea salt to Australian lake salt (super salty) to red sea salt from Peru. Like wine, artisan salt showcases *terroir*—well, not quite *terroir* since that refers to the flavor of the earth, and salt is harvested from water—but the flavor of the place it comes from. Have fun tasting all sorts of salts and seeing what you like best. Find out what salts your favorite gourmet market stocks, and look online at artisansalt.com, saltistry.com (which also sells some killer sea-salt caramels), salttraders.com, and saltworks.us. Become a salt snob—salt is the new black. Or something like that.

little treats

salted caramels

MAKES 40 TO 50 PIECES

I have gone through phases when I am seriously addicted to salted caramels and need to get a daily fix. The beauty is that it doesn't take much to ease the craving—these are perfect little bites of goodness that satisfy. Not many recipes in this book call for a candy thermometer, but I do recommend using one here. If you don't get the caramel hot enough, or if you cook it too long, it won't turn out right. (I know—I've messed up plenty of batches. But don't worry; if it doesn't set for you and stays soft, it makes a yummy sauce for ice cream.) With a thermometer, though, you take the guesswork and uncertainty out of the process.

1 cup heavy cream
5 tablespoons unsalted butter, cut into pieces
½ teaspoon pure vanilla extract
1 teaspoon fine sea salt
1½ cups sugar
2 tablespoons light corn syrup
¼ cup water
1 teaspoon *fleur de sel*

1 Line the bottom and sides of an 8-inch square baking dish with parchment paper, then lightly butter the parchment.

2 Combine the cream, butter, vanilla, and sea salt in a small saucepan and bring to a boil over medium heat. Boil for about 4 minutes, then remove it from the heat and set aside.

3 In a heavy medium-size saucepan, combine the sugar, corn syrup, and water and bring to a boil over medium heat, stirring until the sugar is completely dissolved. If there are any sugar crystals on the side of the pan, brush them down with a damp pastry brush. Once the sugar is dissolved, boil without stirring—swirling the pan occasionally to keep it cooking evenly—until it's a light amber color and the candy thermometer registers 340°F, about 7 minutes.

4 Turn the heat down to medium-low, carefully stir in the cream mixture (it will foam up a lot), and simmer, stirring often, until the liquid is 246°F on the candy thermometer, 6 to 8 minutes. The temperature may hover in the 200° to 220°F range for a while, and then it will start to increase pretty quickly, so watch it carefully.

5 Stir in the *fleur de sel*, then pour the caramel into the prepared baking dish (don't scrape the saucepan or you might get some burned bits that are stuck to the bottom); let cool for at least 3 hours. Cut the caramel into approximately 1-inch squares and wrap each square in waxed paper or aluminum foil. The caramels will keep in an airtight container at room temperature for up to 1 week.

> **SWEET IDEA!**
> Dip the cooled caramels into melted milk chocolate or dark chocolate and garnish with a few flecks of *fleur de sel*. Let the chocolate set firmly before serving.

bittersweet chocolate truffles

When I see a chocolate truffle garnished with a grain of salt, I have to try it. Adding a touch of salt to good chocolate in a simple recipe makes a world of difference. It brings out the complex flavors of the chocolate and makes the whole experience more satisfying. Once you've tried it, regular chocolate truffles will seem bland by comparison. This is a very simple truffle recipe with a bit of fine sea salt added to the truffle mixture and a large crystal of coarse salt on top—to look pretty and for a tiny extra kick of saltiness.

8 ounces good-quality bittersweet chocolate, chopped
½ cup heavy cream
¼ teaspoon fine sea salt
2 tablespoons pure vanilla extract
½ cup cocoa powder, sifted
About 30 crystals coarse sea salt

1 Put the chocolate in a heatproof bowl. Bring the cream almost to a boil in a small saucepan over medium heat, then pour it immediately over the chocolate. Let stand for 4 to 5 minutes to melt the chocolate.

2 When the chocolate is melted, add the fine sea salt and whisk gently until smooth. Add the vanilla and whisk gently to incorporate completely. Cover loosely and refrigerate until firm, at least 2 hours.

3 Using a teaspoon or melon baller, scoop about 1 teaspoon of the chocolate mixture and roll into a ¾-inch round truffle. Roll the truffle in cocoa powder and gently press 1 crystal of coarse salt into the top of the truffle to secure it. Place on a plate or in a container, and continue until all the truffle mixture has been used.

4 Return the truffles to the refrigerator to chill until firm, at least 20 minutes. The truffles will keep in an airtight container in the refrigerator for up to 1 week. Serve chilled or at room temperature.

nana rodda's peanut butter fudge

MAKES 40 TO 50 PIECES

A few of my favorite recipes in this book are adaptations of recipes that come from my mom (I call her Mom), and from her mom (I called her Nana Banana). This one comes from Nana's mom, my great-grandmother, whom we always called Nana Rodda. As Mom says, it's a classic: smooth, creamy, and satisfying. A little bite goes a long way.

2 cups sugar
½ cup whole milk
Heaping ¼ cup creamy peanut butter (regular, not natural)
½ cup (1 stick) unsalted butter
½ teaspoon fine sea salt

1 Combine the sugar and milk in a heavy, medium-size saucepan. Bring to a boil over medium-high heat and boil for about 3 minutes, until a candy thermometer registers 235°F.

2 Add the peanut butter, butter, and salt and stir vigorously with a wooden spoon until thick, 7 to 10 minutes. Pour into an 8-inch square ungreased pan, and let cool completely before cutting into about 1-inch squares for serving. The fudge will keep in an airtight container for up to 1 week.

perfectly imperfect pecan pralines

Every year, I meet up with four of my best friends from way back when (Katie, Hillary, Beth, and Amie) for a girls' weekend. Last year we went to Charleston, South Carolina, and we happened to be there when the Charleston Food + Wine Festival was going on. (Charleston is a phenomenal food city.) Of course I dragged them to the festival with me, not that they minded too much. It was there that I became obsessed with authentic Southern pralines. I sampled at least a dozen varieties—I was not hungry for dinner that night—and then played with recipes at home. This simple version, spiked with a little bourbon, is my favorite. Making pralines becomes incredibly easy when you skip the step of trying to form them into perfect 2½-inch rounds (as they do in the South) but instead spread the whole mixture onto a parchment-lined baking sheet and break it up into bites once it's cool.

1½ cups sugar
½ cup heavy cream
2 tablespoons unsalted butter
½ teaspoon fine sea salt
2 teaspoons molasses
1½ tablespoons bourbon (or 1 teaspoon pure vanilla extract)
1 cup lightly toasted pecan halves (page 13)

1 Line a baking sheet with parchment paper.

2 In a medium-size saucepan, combine the sugar, cream, butter, salt, molasses, and bourbon and bring to a boil over medium-high heat, stirring frequently with a wooden spoon. After it starts to boil, boil for 6 minutes, stirring occasionally.

3 Remove the pan from the heat and let it cool just until the mixture completely stops bubbling. Add the pecan halves and stir them in well, then quickly pour the mixture onto the baking sheet and spread it out as much as you can. (It will get thick quickly while you're doing this—so this is the time to remember that it doesn't have to be perfect!)

4 Let cool completely, then break the praline into bite-size pieces (you get to decide what "bite-size" means . . . and snack on the little shards that don't measure up). The pralines will keep in an airtight container for up to 1 week.

almond **brittle**

MAKES ABOUT 3 CUPS

This recipe was loosely inspired by See's peanut brittle, an addictive treat that my friends Sean and Sophie introduced me to late one night after a dinner party. I knew right away it was the salty-sweet combination that made it so ridiculously good. I wanted something like it in this book, so I thought about other nuts that might work. My two favorite nuts are almonds and cashews. My husband, Will, loves almonds, too, and I love any excuse to use almond extract. So almonds won, and I'm glad they did. I won't say this is better than See's (that would be tough), but it's different and unique and at least equally good. And it's sooooo easy. You just have to keep an eye on it while it's cooking, which doesn't take too long. And then you have to resist the urge to eat it while it's still piping hot.

2 tablespoons unsalted butter
2 cups sugar
¼ cup water
1½ teaspoons pure almond extract
¾ teaspoon fine sea salt
1 cup slivered almonds
½ teaspoon baking soda

1 Line a large rimmed baking sheet with aluminum foil, then grease the foil with 1 tablespoon of the butter.

2 Combine the sugar, water, almond extract, and salt in a medium-size saucepan over medium-high heat. Stir to combine well, then let the mixture come to a boil without stirring it. Let it cook until the sugar starts to caramelize and turn a very light golden brown color, about 10 minutes. (Watch and smell it carefully starting around the 7-minute mark—don't let it burn because the pan will be hard to clean and the brittle will have an unappealing taste and texture.)

3 Stir in the almonds, then stir in the remaining 1 tablespoon butter and the baking soda, being sure to distribute them evenly (the mixture will foam up at this point).

4 Pour the mixture onto the prepared baking sheet and, working quickly with a rubber spatula or wooden spoon, spread it out so you have a uniform thickness, aiming for less than ¼ inch thick (and as thin as you can get it).

5 Let it cool at room temperature for a few minutes, then put the pan in the refrigerator to cool completely. Break up the brittle into pieces (and try not to scarf the whole recipe down yourself). It will keep in an airtight container for up to 10 days.

SWEET IDEAS!

✳ **Dip the cooled almond brittle pieces halfway or completely into melted chocolate (I like bittersweet for this) and let them cool completely on a clean baking sheet.**
✳ **Stick a long, thin shard of brittle into a piece of cake or a mousse for an elegant garnish.**
✳ **Break the brittle into small pieces and serve over ice cream with hot fudge. Or break the brittle into smaller pieces and mix it into vanilla ice cream (like they do at mix-in ice cream parlors) and you'll have "homemade" almond brittle ice cream.**
✳ **Grind the brittle into crumbs with a rolling pin and work it into the topping for a fruit crisp.**

salty-sweet s'mores

MAKES 24 S'MORES

S'mores are among my all-time favorite sweets. They taste best when the marshmallows are toasted outdoors over an open flame, of course, but that's not always an option. When you're in the mood for something resembling that great campfire s'mores taste, but that you can make in your kitchen, try these gooey bites. Use the best marshmallows you can find for this—look for handmade artisan marshmallows at a gourmet shop or a good grocery store.

12 whole graham crackers, broken into quarters
9 ounces milk chocolate, broken into 24 pieces
Fleur de sel
8 to 12 gourmet marshmallows, cut into ½-inch cubes

1 Preheat the broiler.

2 Arrange 24 of the graham cracker quarters on a baking sheet lined with parchment paper. Top each with a piece of chocolate. Sprinkle the chocolate with *fleur de sel* and top with a marshmallow cube.

3 Broil just until the marshmallow is browned on top—this will happen quickly, in just 1 to 2 minutes, depending on your broiler.

4 Remove the s'mores from the oven and top them with the remaining 24 graham crackers. Press down gently, let cool for 1 minute, and serve immediately.

black-and-white almond bark

I love making chocolate bark around the holidays, sometimes with peppermint, sometimes with nuts. It's easy to do and it looks impressive—definitely gift-worthy. This is a year-round-appropriate version of bark, and it's delectable with a hint of salt.

8 ounces dark chocolate
½ teaspoon fine sea salt
8 ounces white chocolate
½ teaspoon pure almond extract
½ cup plus 1 tablespoon crushed almonds
About ¼ teaspoon grinder sea salt

1 Line a rimmed baking sheet with parchment paper.

2 Melt the dark chocolate in a heatproof bowl set over simmering water or in the top of a double boiler. When it's melted, stir in the fine sea salt and distribute evenly. Use a rubber spatula or the back of a wooden spoon to spread the mixture about ⅛ inch thick on the parchment-lined sheet. Let cool in the refrigerator for 20 minutes.

3 Melt the white chocolate in a heatproof bowl set over simmering water or in the top of a double boiler. When it's melted, remove from the heat to let it cool slightly but not too much, 3 to 5 minutes, and quickly stir in the almond extract and ½ cup of the almonds.

4 Spread the white chocolate mixture over the cooled dark chocolate. Combine the grinder sea salt with the remaining 1 tablespoon almonds and sprinkle over the white chocolate before it hardens. Let cool in the refrigerator for 45 minutes or at room temperature for 2 hours. Break into pieces and serve, or store in an airtight container at room temperature for up to 1 week.

sweet and salty pecans

Quick and easy to make, these sweet and salty nuts are great for snacking, serving with ice cream, mixing into cookie recipes, or even using on top of salads.

2 tablespoons packed light brown sugar
¼ cup granulated sugar
½ teaspoon fine sea salt
2 tablespoons water
1 cup pecan pieces

1 Combine the brown sugar, granulated sugar, salt, and water in a small bowl; stir to dissolve.

2 Place the pecans in a large skillet over medium heat. Pour the sugar mixture over the pecans and stir to coat. Continue stirring as the mixture heats up and starts to bubble; let it cook until the moisture is almost gone, 5 to 7 minutes. Keep an eye on it and don't let the water cook off completely.

3 Remove from the heat and spread on a baking sheet to cool. Let cool completely before using in recipes—or eat out of hand as soon as they're cool enough! The nuts will keep in an airtight container for up to 1 week.

SWEET IDEAS!

* Replace the pecans with another kind of nut you love—walnuts, almonds, peanuts—or a mix of nuts.
* Use the pecans as a garnish for a chocolate dessert, or stick one on top of a frosted cupcake.

dark chocolate and sea salt crostini

MAKES 18 CROSTINI

I love savory crostini. They're the perfect all-purpose appetizer: little toasty slices of baguette topped with just about anything you can think of. My dream meal is a bunch of different kinds of crostini, maybe a salad, and of course a salty-sweet treat. There's a restaurant in New York City called Fig & Olive Kitchen and Tasting Bar that has lots of crostini on the menu—and you can order an assortment of flavors all on one plate. With a glass of wine, it's perfect. Over a platter one night with friends, I found myself wishing we could have more crostini for dessert. Hey, if savory crostini are that good, why not a sweet version? This one is so good, and so simple. Just good bread, good chocolate, and a little sprinkling of coarse sea salt—just enough to highlight the fabulous flavor in the chocolate. Speaking of which, use excellent-quality chocolate here.

1 baguette, cut into eighteen ¼-inch-thick slices
6 ounces dark or bittersweet chocolate, broken into
   18 bite-size squares
Grinder sea salt

1 Preheat the oven to 350°F.

2 Arrange the baguette slices in a single layer on a baking sheet. Place a square of chocolate on top of each baguette slice.

3 Bake for about 7 minutes, or until the chocolate is soft and melted but is still in its original shape.

4 Remove the baking sheet from the oven and quickly sprinkle the chocolate with a very light dusting of sea salt. Serve immediately.

old-fashioned kettle corn

Popcorn with salt and sugar sounds simple, but it's addictive. This is one of the original salty sweets. I first tried it while watching a pro tennis match. Lindsay Davenport was playing Jennifer Capriati. I love watching tennis, and I was in the second row, but I was so distracted by the kettle corn that I don't even remember who won. The kettle corn was that good. This is fun to give guests at parties after dinner instead of a heavy dessert, especially if there's a big game or a movie to be watched.

¼ cup canola oil
½ cup popcorn kernels
¼ cup sugar
1 teaspoon fine sea salt

1 Heat the oil over medium-high heat in a large pot with a tight-fitting lid. Place 4 or 5 popcorn kernels in the oil in the pan and cover with the lid. When those kernels pop, add the rest of the popcorn kernels.

2 Quickly shake the pan to distribute the kernels. When the oil sizzles, sprinkle the sugar and salt over the kernels. Cover the pan and shake the kernels for about 3 minutes, until most of them have popped and the popping slows. (Don't wait for every kernel to pop or you may scorch your popcorn.) Remove from the heat. Taste and season with a bit more salt, if desired. Serve immediately.

dark chocolate–covered pretzels

Chocolate-covered pretzels are one of the quintessential salty-sweet combinations. Make them a little less sweet and a little more sophisticated with great-quality dark chocolate.

6 ounces dark or bittersweet chocolate, chopped
1 tablespoon heavy cream
2 cups mini pretzels

1 Line a large baking sheet (or two small ones) with parchment paper.

2 Melt the chocolate in a heatproof bowl over simmering water or in the top of a double boiler. Remove the chocolate from the heat and stir in the cream until completely incorporated and smooth.

3 Use tongs to dip the pretzels into the chocolate until well coated. Let the excess chocolate drip back into the bowl, then let the pretzels dry on the parchment-lined baking sheet. Refrigerate for about 30 minutes, until the chocolate sets. The pretzels will keep in an airtight container at room temperature for up to 5 days.

SWEET IDEA!
Before the chocolate sets, dip each pretzel into shredded toasted coconut or ground nuts.

chocolate-coconut mini candy bars

I love chocolate and I love coconut, so I wanted to come up with a recipe for a confection featuring both of those flavors. This simple, no-bake concoction was a surprise hit—it couldn't be much easier, and Will (my husband, who tasted just about everything in this book) says they are one of his all-time favorites. They are rich and intense, so keep the pieces small. I think they'd be great to serve after a lunch or dinner party. Because there are so few ingredients, it's important to use the best you can find: Think organic coconut, great salt, and super-high-quality organic chocolate.

1½ cups unsweetened shredded coconut
½ teaspoon Maldon salt (or another flaked sea salt)
⅓ cup sweetened condensed milk
4 ounces bittersweet chocolate, melted

1 Line two 5 x 9-inch loaf pans with parchment paper, letting the ends overlap the edges of the pans.

2 In a medium-size bowl, mix together the coconut, salt, and condensed milk until thoroughly combined. Divide the mixture between the pans and spread it in an even layer with a rubber spatula. Refrigerate for about 10 minutes.

3 Spread the melted chocolate over the chilled coconut layer, dividing it evenly between the pans and distributing it uniformly over the coconut. Chill until just firm, about 5 minutes.

4 Remove the chilled chocolate-coconut layers from the pans, peel off the parchment paper, and firmly press the two coconut sides together, forming a chocolate-coconut sandwich. Cut into bite-size pieces (about 1-inch squares) and keep covered and refrigerated until ready to serve. The candies keep in the refrigerator for up to 4 days.

decadent hot cocoa

Sometimes you need a cup of cocoa. And when you do, may I suggest making yourself a fabulous European-style hot cocoa—from scratch—instead of using a processed mix? Use excellent cocoa powder here, for sure. I like Green & Black's Organic. Using brown sugar instead of granulated sugar in hot cocoa is a trick I learned from the amazing pastry chef Gale Gand. The flavor it gives is fantastic, and more interesting. This reminds me of the cocoa I get at a phenomenal café called Boulettes Larder in San Francisco. The tiny dash of salt and sprinkling of *fleur de sel* make this version even more intense than that.

¾ cup milk
1 tablespoon plus 1 teaspoon unsweetened cocoa powder
2 teaspoons packed light brown sugar
Pinch of fine sea salt
1 drop pure vanilla extract
Fleur de sel

1 Bring the milk to a simmer in a small saucepan over medium heat.

2 In a small bowl, stir together the cocoa powder, brown sugar, and sea salt. Stir 2 teaspoons of the hot milk into the cocoa mixture to make a smooth paste.

3 Transfer the cocoa paste to the saucepan with the remaining milk and let simmer for 2 minutes over very low heat, making sure it doesn't boil. Remove from the heat and add the vanilla.

4 Pour into a mug and sprinkle with a few flakes of *fleur de sel*. Serve immediately.

sweet cornbread with honey butter

MAKES ABOUT 16 PIECES

I can't be left alone with good cornbread—I might devour it all. To me it feels like a decadent treat, with a texture similar to cake but a little less sweet and a little more buttery. To add to the richness of it all, serve this cornbread with soft honey butter flecked with coarse salt. Use great-quality local honey and organic butter—you will taste the difference.

1 cup all-purpose flour
1 cup cornmeal
¼ cup packed light brown sugar
1 tablespoon baking powder
1 teaspoon fine sea salt
2 large eggs, lightly beaten
1 cup milk
¼ cup (½ stick) melted and slightly cooled
   unsalted butter
Honey Butter (recipe follows)

1 Preheat the oven to 400°F. Butter the bottom and ½ inch up the sides of a 9-inch square baking dish.

2 In a medium-size bowl, combine the flour, cornmeal, brown sugar, baking powder, and salt, and stir to combine well. Make a well in the center of the mixture.

3 In a separate bowl, whisk together the eggs, milk, and melted butter. Pour the egg mixture into the well in the dry ingredients and mix until the dry ingredients are just moistened.

4 Transfer the batter to the buttered baking dish and bake for 20 to 25 minutes, until the top is light golden and springs back gently when you press it. Let cool in the pan on a wire rack. Cut into approximately 2-inch squares and serve with Honey Butter.

honey butter

MAKES ABOUT ⅔ CUP

½ cup (1 stick) unsalted butter, softened
2 tablespoons light honey
½ teaspoon grinder sea salt
Pinch of coarse sea salt

1 Combine the butter, honey, and grinder sea salt in a small bowl and mix with a wooden spoon until thoroughly combined.

2 Press the honey butter into a ramekin, smooth the top, and sprinkle lightly with coarse sea salt. Serve at room temperature.

> SWEET IDEA!
> Make a "brownie sundae" with cornbread by topping a square of warm Sweet Cornbread with a scoop of vanilla ice cream or Nantucket Sea Salt Ice Cream (page 114), adding some sliced fresh peaches, and drizzling with Snappy Butterscotch Sauce (page 128) or Drunken Sauce (page 134).

cocoa nib and dried cherry granola

MAKES ABOUT 7 CUPS

Granola is one of my favorite things to make. Once you know a basic recipe, you can vary it in countless ways. Use different kinds of dried fruits, add different nuts, and play around with the ratio of sweeteners. This is a delicious version of my go-to recipe, which has no oil and just 3 tablespoons of butter. The butter, with the addition of sea salt, gives it a rich and satisfying flavor. Cocoa nibs are the essence of deep, intense chocolateness—they are roasted cacao beans separated from their husks, and they're great with dried cherries. I love this take on the chocolate-cherry combo.

½ cup honey
½ cup pure maple syrup
¼ cup packed light brown sugar
3 tablespoons unsalted butter
1 teaspoon pure vanilla extract
4 cups old-fashioned or quick-cooking rolled oats
  (not instant)
¾ cup unsweetened shredded coconut
1 teaspoon fine sea salt
1 cup dried cherries
¼ cup cocoa nibs

1 Preheat the oven to 325°F. Line a rimmed baking sheet with parchment paper.

2 Combine the honey, maple syrup, brown sugar, butter, and vanilla in a medium-size saucepan. Bring to a boil over medium heat, being careful not to let the mixture boil over, then reduce the heat and simmer for about 5 minutes, stirring often.

3 Mix the oats, coconut, and salt in a large bowl. Pour the hot honey mixture over the oat mixture, stir to coat thoroughly, and spread evenly on the baking sheet.

4 Bake for 15 minutes, stirring occasionally, then add the cherries and cocoa nibs and bake for another 15 to 17 minutes, stirring occasionally, until golden brown. Remove the granola from the oven and let it cool completely. The granola will keep in an airtight container at room temperature for up to 2 weeks.

SWEET IDEAS!
✳ **Sprinkle warm granola over ice cream (try it with Bittersweet Chocolate Ice Cream, page 117).**
✳ **Replace the dried cherries with chopped dried apricots and add ¼ cup white chocolate chips after baking and cooling.**

cookies and bars

chocolate chip cookies

MAKES 30 TO 40 COOKIES

I've made a lot of chocolate chip cookies. *A lot.* And I thought I had tweaked and refined my basic recipe to mouthwatering perfection. Then I tried sprinkling the cookies with grinder sea salt, and I realized that I'd been missing out. You don't need much salt to put your cookies over the edge, but if you make them like this your friends will start begging you to make them all the time. When I make cookies I like to use a small ice cream scoop or two spoons to drop the dough onto the baking sheets. It minimizes mess and ensures your cookies will be of uniform size, making for better baking results.

2¼ cups all-purpose flour
1 teaspoon baking soda
1 teaspoon fine sea salt
¾ cup (1½ sticks) unsalted butter, softened
½ cup granulated sugar
1 cup packed light brown sugar
1½ teaspoons pure vanilla extract
2 large eggs
2 cups bittersweet chocolate chips or chunks
Grinder sea salt

1 Preheat the oven to 375°F. Line baking sheets with parchment paper.

2 In a medium-size bowl, whisk together the flour, baking soda, and fine sea salt. Set aside.

3 In the bowl of a stand mixer fitted with a paddle attachment, beat the butter with the sugars until creamy. Add the vanilla and beat until thoroughly combined. Beat in the eggs one at a time.

4 Slowly add the flour mixture to the mixer bowl, mixing it in a little at a time, until the flour is well incorporated. Stir in the chocolate chips.

5 Use an ice cream scoop or two spoons to drop balls of dough (about 2 tablespoons each) onto the baking sheets. Bake for 8 to 10 minutes, until set and just golden.

6 Remove the cookies from the oven and immediately sprinkle them with a light dusting of grinder sea salt. Let cool on the baking sheets for about 1 minute, then remove them to a wire rack and let them cool completely. The cookies will keep in an airtight container at room temperature for up to 5 days.

chocolate oatmeal cookies

MAKES 30 TO 40 COOKIES

I didn't think I could like any kind of cookie better than chocolate chip. Then I stumbled upon samples of thick, rustic-looking chocolate-oatmeal cookies dusted with sea salt at a gourmet shop in Boston called South End Formaggio. The cookies are called Salty Oats and are made by a Cape Cod bakery called Kayak Cookies. One bite and I was hooked—totally, completely addicted. This is my interpretation of those cookies. Whenever I make them, they are gone in a flash.

2 cups all-purpose flour
⅔ cup unsweetened cocoa powder
1 teaspoon baking soda
1 teaspoon fine sea salt
¾ cup (1½ sticks) unsalted butter, softened
½ cup granulated sugar
1 cup packed light brown sugar
1 teaspoon pure vanilla extract
2 large eggs
1 cup old-fashioned or quick-cooking rolled oats
  (not instant)
1 cup semisweet or bittersweet chocolate chips
½ cup unsweetened shredded coconut
Grinder sea salt

1 Preheat the oven to 350°F. Line baking sheets with parchment paper.

2 Thoroughly combine the flour, cocoa powder, baking soda, and fine sea salt in a medium-size bowl.

3 In the bowl of a stand mixer fitted with a paddle attachment, beat the butter, sugars, and vanilla until the mixture is creamy. Add the eggs one at a time, beating or stirring thoroughly after each egg.

4 Stir in the flour mixture in 4 to 5 increments, combining well after each addition. Stir in the oats, chocolate chips, and coconut.

5 Use an ice cream scoop or two spoons to drop balls of dough (about 2 tablespoons each) onto the baking sheets. Sprinkle each ball very lightly with grinder sea salt.

6 Bake for about 11 minutes, until the tops have just started to crack. While the cookies are still on the sheet, sprinkle them again very lightly with grinder sea salt. Let them cool on the baking sheets for about 1 minute, then remove them to a wire rack and let them cool completely. The cookies will keep in an airtight container at room temperature for up to 5 days.

SWEET IDEAS!
* Replace the chocolate chips with white chocolate chips.
* Place a scoop of vanilla ice cream or Almond Ice Cream (page 119) between two cookies to make an ice cream sandwich.

nantucket cookies

As far as I know, this isn't the official cookie of Nantucket, but maybe it should be. It features cranberries (a crop that has been grown on Nantucket since 1857), white chocolate (to contrast with the tartness of the cranberries), and a sprinkling of sea salt (Nantucket is an island 30 miles off the coast . . . salty sea breezes blow every day . . . you get it). Since Nantucket is one of my favorite places on the planet, I hereby dedicate this cookie to it.

2¼ cups all-purpose flour

1 teaspoon baking soda

1 teaspoon fine sea salt

⅔ cup (1 stick plus 1⅓ tablespoons) unsalted butter, softened

¾ cup granulated sugar

¾ cup packed light brown sugar

1½ teaspoons pure vanilla extract

2 large eggs

1 cup dried cranberries, preferably unsweetened

1 cup white chocolate chips or chunks

Grinder sea salt

1 Preheat the oven to 375°F. Line baking sheets with parchment paper.

2 In a medium-size bowl, whisk together the flour, baking soda, and fine sea salt. Set aside.

3 In the bowl of a stand mixer fitted with a paddle attachment, beat the butter with the sugars until creamy. Add the vanilla and beat until thoroughly combined. Beat in the eggs one at a time.

4 Slowly add the flour mixture to the mixer bowl, mixing it in a little at a time, until the flour is well incorporated. Stir in the cranberries and white chocolate chips.

5 Use an ice cream scoop or two spoons to drop balls of dough (about 2 tablespoons each) onto the baking sheets. Bake for 8 to 10 minutes, until set and just golden.

6 Remove the cookies from the oven and immediately sprinkle them with a light dusting of grinder sea salt. Let cool on the baking sheets for about 1 minute, then remove them to a wire rack and let them cool completely. The cookies will keep in an airtight container at room temperature for up to 5 days.

SWEET IDEA!
Try bittersweet chocolate chips in place of the white chocolate chips for a less sweet, more intense cookie.

peanut butter cookies

I like peanut butter cookies that are intensely peanut buttery. Bland versions are always disappointing. With this recipe, there's no getting away from the peanut butter—it's the star ingredient, and there's little else to distract from it. A mix of dark brown and granulated sugars caramelizes beautifully and becomes nice and chewy. The result of this almost flour-free recipe is closer to a macaroon than a cookie—airy and definitely not leaden, the way some peanut butter cookies can turn out. Chopped salted peanuts lend interesting texture, more peanut flavor, and a bit of extra saltiness that contrasts nicely with the caramel sweetness.

1 tablespoon all-purpose flour
1 teaspoon baking soda
½ teaspoon fine sea salt
1 cup creamy peanut butter (regular, not natural)
½ cup granulated sugar
½ cup packed dark brown sugar
1 large egg, lightly beaten
3 tablespoons finely chopped salted peanuts

1 Preheat the oven to 350°F.

2 In a small bowl, combine the flour, baking soda, and sea salt.

3 In a medium-size bowl, stir together the peanut butter, granulated sugar, brown sugar, and the flour mixture until well combined. Stir in the beaten egg until well incorporated, and then stir in the peanuts.

4 Roll the dough into 1-inch balls and place them 3 inches apart on parchment-lined baking sheets. Flatten the balls slightly with the back of a fork, making a grid pattern (once the cookies are baked, the pattern won't be quite as obvious as it is on traditional peanut butter cookies, but the traditionalist in me enjoys the effect, and flattening the dough a little before baking helps them to be more consistent in texture and doneness throughout).

5 Bake for about 12 minutes, until set and just slightly browned. (Overbaking these will lead to very crispy edges, which aren't bad, but I like them when they're a little softer.) Let cool on the baking sheets for about 1 minute, then transfer to a wire rack to cool completely.

lemon sugar cookies with zesty lime salt

MAKES ABOUT 30 COOKIES

I love the idea of a margarita. Thanks to an unfortunate experience with tequila one night during college, however, I don't drink them. Believe me, I've tried, because the lemony, limey drink with the glass rimmed in salt always looks so good, especially in summer. Ah, well. Here's a cookie that features what I imagine to be the best elements of the cocktail I must avoid, yet still crave.

2 cups all-purpose flour
¾ teaspoon fine sea salt
1 cup (2 sticks) unsalted butter, softened
1 cup sugar
1 large egg yolk
1 tablespoon fresh lemon juice
1 teaspoon lemon zest
Zest of 1 lime

1 Combine the flour and ½ teaspoon of the salt in a medium-size bowl and mix well.

2 In the bowl of a stand mixer fitted with a paddle attachment, cream the butter for 1 minute, then add ¾ cup of the sugar and beat on medium-high speed for 3 minutes, until the mixture is light and fluffy.

3 Add the egg yolk, lemon juice, and lemon zest and beat for 2 more minutes. Slowly add the flour mixture and mix on low speed until the dough comes together.

4 Combine the lime zest, the remaining ¼ cup sugar, and the remaining ¼ teaspoon sea salt in a shallow dish or on a plate (for rolling).

5 Roll the dough into logs 1½ to 2 inches in diameter, then roll the logs in the lime zest mixture. Wrap the logs in plastic wrap and refrigerate for 30 minutes to 1 hour.

6 Preheat the oven to 350°F. Line baking sheets with parchment paper.

7 Slice the chilled logs into ¼-inch-thick circles and place on baking sheets. Bake for 9 to 11 minutes, or until just lightly browned on the bottom. Let cool on the baking sheets for about 1 minute, then transfer to a wire rack to cool completely. The cookies will keep in an airtight container for up to 3 days.

lavender fleur de sel shortbread

There's a little market near my house in San Francisco that stocks an eclectic assortment of gourmet crackers, olive oils, prepared foods, and baked goods. One day, in dire need of a treat, I wandered in there, wondering if I would find anything to make me feel better (it was one of those days). And there on the counter near the door was a glass cookie jar filled with lavender *fleur de sel* shortbread. I had a feeling that would work as a mood elevator, and I was right. The flavor combination is fantastic, and lavender is very soothing. Aaah. I came up with this recipe so I could make them for myself whenever I need to de-stress. Look for culinary lavender at gourmet stores, or purchase one of my favorite kinds, from Matanzas Creek Winery in Santa Rosa, California, online at matanzascreek.com.

1 cup all-purpose flour
½ teaspoon fine sea salt
⅓ cup sugar
2 teaspoons chopped dried lavender blossoms
½ cup (1 stick) unsalted butter, softened
1 teaspoon pure vanilla extract
Fleur de sel

1 Sift the flour and fine sea salt together in a small bowl.

2 Combine the sugar and lavender in the bowl of a stand mixer fitted with a paddle attachment. Mix for 15 to 20 seconds to combine. Add the butter and mix until combined. Mix in the vanilla. Add the flour mixture to the butter mixture and mix on low speed until it forms a soft dough.

3 Shape the dough into a disk, wrap tightly in plastic wrap, and refrigerate for 20 to 30 minutes.

4 Line a baking sheet with parchment paper. Roll out the dough to ¼ inch thick and cut it into 1½- to 2½-inch shapes (circles, squares, or hearts) using a cookie cutter or knife. Place the shapes on the baking sheet and place the baking sheet in the freezer for 15 minutes, until the dough is stiff.

5 Meanwhile, preheat the oven to 350°F.

6 Bake the cookies for 12 to 15 minutes, or until the edges turn golden brown. Sprinkle the cookies lightly with *fleur de sel* as soon as they come out of the oven. Let cool for 5 minutes on the baking sheet, then transfer them to a wire rack to cool completely. The shortbread keeps for up to 5 days in an airtight container.

SWEET IDEA!
Add a hint of lemon flavor to these cookies by mixing in a teaspoon of grated lemon zest along with the vanilla extract, or by replacing the vanilla with lemon extract.

snickerdoodles

MAKES 30 TO 40 COOKIES

Snickerdoodles are definitely a cookie I associate with being a kid. My older sister, Jen, always loved them—which in my mind made them the coolest cookie around. (That might be a rare perception of a snickerdoodle.) I still think they're cool, and even cooler when there's a little sea salt added to the cinnamon sugar they are rolled in before baking.

2½ cups all-purpose flour
1 teaspoon baking soda
2 teaspoons cream of tartar
½ teaspoon fine sea salt
1 cup (2 sticks) unsalted butter, softened
1¾ cups sugar
2 large eggs
1 teaspoon pure vanilla extract
2 teaspoons ground cinnamon
½ teaspoon grinder sea salt

1 Sift together the flour, baking soda, cream of tartar, and fine sea salt.

2 In the bowl of a stand mixer fitted with a paddle attachment, cream together the butter and 1½ cups of the sugar for 2 minutes. Beat in the eggs, then mix in the vanilla. Slowly add the flour mixture to the butter mixture and mix until well blended. Refrigerate the dough for at least 30 minutes.

3 Preheat the oven to 400°F. Line baking sheets with parchment paper.

4 In a shallow bowl, combine the remaining ¼ cup sugar, the cinnamon, and the grinder sea salt. Roll the chilled dough into 1½-inch balls and roll each ball in the cinnamon-sugar-salt mixture. Arrange them 3 inches apart on the baking sheets.

5 Bake for 10 to 12 minutes, until the edges are light golden brown. Let cool on the baking sheets for 2 minutes, then transfer them to a wire rack to cool completely. The cookies will keep in an airtight container for up to 5 days.

butterscotch **brownies**

When I was growing up, my mom always made chocolate brownies from a mix, but butterscotch brownies (blondies, in the vernacular of some households) were made from scratch. So simple—a warm, oozing combination of butter and brown sugar mixed with dry ingredients and eggs and spiked with vanilla and nuts—and so delicious. Adding a little salt to the butterscotch heightens the flavor and makes these even more mouthwatering. They're often made with walnuts (and you could certainly substitute walnuts here), but I like them best with little bits of chopped pecans.

2 cups all-purpose flour

1¼ teaspoons fine sea salt

1 teaspoon baking powder

¼ teaspoon baking soda

2 cups packed dark brown sugar

10 tablespoons (1¼ sticks) unsalted butter, melted

2 large eggs

2 teaspoons pure vanilla extract

1 cup chopped toasted pecans (page 13)

1 Preheat the oven to 325°F. Butter and flour a 9 x 13-inch glass or ceramic baking pan.

2 Combine the flour, ¾ teaspoon of the salt, the baking powder, and the baking soda in a medium-size bowl.

3 In the bowl of a stand mixer fitted with a whisk attachment, whisk together the brown sugar and the remaining ½ teaspoon salt so the salt is evenly distributed. Pour in the melted butter and whisk until well blended. Whisk in the eggs and the vanilla.

4 Slowly add the flour mixture to the bowl, whisking until it's just incorporated. Fold in the pecans.

5 Spread the batter into the baking pan, distributing it evenly all the way to the edges. Bake for 30 to 35 minutes, until the batter is completely set and the edges are just starting to brown. (A tester won't come out totally clean at this point—it should have some goop on it.)

6 Let cool in the pan on a wire rack for 10 minutes, then chill the pan in the refrigerator for 30 minutes to 1 hour to help the inside set before cutting. Cut the brownies into squares and serve. The brownies will keep in an airtight container at room temperature for up to 3 days, or for up to 1 month in the freezer, wrapped tightly in two layers of plastic wrap.

SWEET IDEA!
Before baking, sprinkle the batter with ¾ cup chocolate chips and then a light dusting of grinder sea salt on top to enhance the chocolate flavor—which at the same time keeps the chocolate from overpowering the salty-sweet balance. You could also stir the chips into the batter, or sprinkle chocolate chips and salt over just half the pan, keeping the other half chocolate-free.

toffee cookies with **dark chocolate glaze**

MAKES 20 TO 24 COOKIES

I first made these cookies seven or eight years ago, when I was just starting to learn about the merits of really, really good chocolate. And wow, do these showcase what a difference good chocolate can make. The cookies are sweet and rich, the perfect foil for an intense layer of dark chocolate.

1 cup (2 sticks) unsalted butter, softened
1 cup packed dark brown sugar
2 large egg yolks
2 cups all-purpose flour
1 teaspoon fine sea salt
4 ounces bittersweet chocolate
¼ cup chopped toasted pecans (page 13)
Fleur de sel

1 Preheat the oven to 350°F. Line baking sheets with parchment paper.

2 In the bowl of a stand mixer fitted with a paddle attachment, cream together the butter and brown sugar. Add the egg yolks one at a time and mix well.

3 Combine the flour and salt in a small bowl, then add the flour mixture to the butter-sugar mixture, mixing until well combined.

4 Shape the dough into a disk, wrap it in plastic wrap, and refrigerate for 10 minutes.

5 Roll out the dough on a lightly floured surface to about ¼ inch thick. Cut out circles with a 2-inch round cutter and place the cookies on the baking sheets.

6 Bake for 11 to 13 minutes, until the edges are golden brown. Let cool completely on the baking sheets.

7 Bring water to a simmer in a double boiler, or set up a heat-proof bowl over a small saucepan with water simmering in the bottom. Melt the chocolate over the simmering water. When the cookies are cool, spread them gently with a thin layer of melted chocolate. Before the chocolate dries, sprinkle lightly with the pecans and a few grains of *fleur de sel*. Let the chocolate set. The cookies will keep in an airtight container at room temperature for up to 3 days.

> **SWEET IDEAS!**
> ✳ Replace the pecans with chopped walnuts, hazelnuts, or almonds.
> ✳ After the bittersweet chocolate sets, drizzle it with a few lines of melted milk or white chocolate.

raspberry **squares**

MAKES 12 LARGE SQUARES

These treats are absolutely simple to make and mouth-wateringly good. Whenever I see a luscious-looking raspberry square at a bakery or gourmet sandwich shop, I want it. A smidgen of sea salt enhances the flavor of the crust and the crumb topping, and while you could certainly use purchased raspberry jam for this (if you can get really good-quality stuff), making your own is easy, and the result is intensely fruity.

1 cup (2 sticks) unsalted butter, softened
⅔ cup confectioners' sugar
2½ cups all-purpose flour
½ teaspoon sea salt
1 cup Gooey Raspberry Jam (recipe follows)

1 Preheat the oven to 350°F.

2 In the bowl of a stand mixer fitted with a paddle attachment, cream the butter and sugar together.

3 Combine the flour and salt in a small bowl, then add the flour mixture to the butter-sugar mixture and mix until combined but still somewhat crumbly.

4 Press about half of the dough into the bottom of a 9 x 13-inch baking pan, distributing it evenly and covering the bottom of the pan thoroughly. Bake for 5 minutes, then spread the jam evenly over the hot bottom crust. Crumble the remaining dough evenly over the jam and pat it down gently.

5 Bake for 20 to 30 minutes, until the topping starts to turn light golden brown. Let cool for at least 15 minutes before cutting and serving. Serve warm or at room temperature. The bars will keep in an airtight container at room temperature for up to 3 days.

gooey raspberry jam

MAKES ABOUT 1 CUP

3 cups fresh raspberries
½ cup sugar
½ teaspoon orange zest (optional)
¼ teaspoon fine sea salt

1 Place the raspberries in a medium-size saucepan and mash
them gently with a fork or a masher. Cook over medium heat for
8 minutes.

2 Turn the heat down to low and stir in the sugar until dissolved.
Stir in the orange zest, if desired, and the salt and cook for another 10 to 12 minutes, until thick. Pour into a heatproof jar and
let cool before using. The jam will keep in an airtight container
in the refrigerator for up to 2 weeks.

SWEET IDEAS!
* Mix ½ cup unsweetened shredded coconut into the dough used for
the topping before sprinkling it over the jam.
* Mix ½ teaspoon almond extract into the butter-sugar mixture before adding the flour, and mix ½ cup chopped almonds into the dough
used for the topping before sprinkling it over the jam.

pecan squares

MAKES ABOUT 24 SQUARES

A whole slice of pecan pie always feels like a little too much to me, but somehow these squares, which have that yummy, nutty, buttery pecan pie flavor (and of which I always end up eating way more than a pie slice's worth), seem just right. They have a buttery shortbread crust and a tasty, gooey topping. For a fantastic dessert, try them warm from the oven with a scoop of Salted Caramel Ice Cream (page 115).

CRUST
⅔ cup confectioners' sugar
2 cups all-purpose flour
½ teaspoon fine sea salt
1 cup (2 sticks) unsalted butter, softened

TOPPING
10 tablespoons (1¼ sticks) unsalted butter, melted
½ cup honey
3 tablespoons heavy cream
½ cup packed dark brown sugar
½ teaspoon *fleur de sel*
4 cups pecans, chopped

1 Preheat the oven to 350°F.

2 To make the crust, sift the confectioners' sugar, flour, and fine sea salt together in a medium-size bowl.

3 Beat the butter until creamy in the bowl of a stand mixer fitted with a paddle attachment. Add the flour-sugar mixture to the butter and mix on low speed until fine crumbs form.

4 Gather the dough into a ball and press it into a 9 x 13-inch baking dish, distributing it as evenly as possible. Bake for about 15 minutes, until it starts to look dry but not browned. Let cool for 10 to 15 minutes.

5 To make the topping, mix the melted butter, honey, cream, brown sugar, and *fleur de sel* together in a medium-size bowl. Stir in the pecans and then spread the topping over the crust. Bake for about 25 more minutes, until set and golden brown. Let cool completely and then cut into squares. The squares will keep in an airtight container at room temperature for up to 3 days.

white chocolate–apricot squares

MAKES 12 LARGE SQUARES

I love all different kinds of fruit squares with shortbread-inspired bases and crumbly toppings. They are terrific when they are super-simple (like the Raspberry Squares on page 56), and it's fun to play with variations on the theme. This version has oats, brown sugar, and white chocolate chips—and the result is a decadent mixture of textures and flavors. Use the best apricot preserves you can find for this.

1 cup (2 sticks) unsalted butter, softened
½ cup packed light brown sugar
1½ cups all-purpose flour
1 cup old-fashioned or quick-cooking rolled oats
  (not instant)
½ teaspoon fine sea salt
1 cup apricot preserves
½ cup white chocolate chips

1 Preheat the oven to 350°F.

2 In the bowl of a stand mixer fitted with a paddle attachment, cream the butter and brown sugar together.

3 Combine the flour, oats, and salt in a small bowl, then add the flour mixture to the butter-sugar mixture and mix until combined but still somewhat crumbly.

4 Press about half of the dough into the bottom of a 9 x 13-inch baking pan, distributing it evenly and covering the bottom of the pan thoroughly. Bake for 5 minutes, then spread the preserves evenly over the bottom crust. Mix the white chocolate chips into the remaining dough, crumble evenly over the jam, and pat down gently.

5 Bake for 20 to 30 minutes, until the topping starts to turn light golden brown. Let cool for at least 15 minutes before cutting and serving. Serve warm or at room temperature. The bars will keep in an airtight container at room temperature for up to 3 days.

SWEET IDEA!
Substitute Gooey Raspberry Jam (page 57) for the apricot preserves if you love the combination of white chocolate and raspberries.

citrus bars

MAKES ABOUT 24 BARS

I'm always happy to see lemon bars at a bridal or baby shower or an afternoon tea—which is where they seem to show up most often. They are especially delicious when the lemon filling is super-citrusy, so that there's a sharp and delicious contrast between that and the simple shortbread crust. This is a twist on lemon bars that features a mix of fresh orange and lemon juices and zests. They are just a tad less tart than traditional lemon bars, making them the perfect foil for the hint of salt sprinkled on top.

CRUST
1 cup (2 sticks) unsalted butter, softened
½ cup granulated sugar
2 cups all-purpose flour
¼ teaspoon fine sea salt

FILLING
6 large eggs
3 cups granulated sugar
Zest of 2 oranges
¾ cup fresh orange juice
Zest of 2 lemons
¼ cup fresh lemon juice
1 cup all-purpose flour

TOPPING
⅓ cup confectioners' sugar
¼ teaspoon *fleur de sel*

1 Preheat the oven to 350°F.

2 To make the crust, combine the butter and sugar in the bowl of a stand mixer fitted with a paddle attachment and beat until creamy.

3 In a separate bowl, whisk together the flour and salt, then mix them into the butter-sugar mixture on low speed until a dough just begins to form.

4 Gather the dough into a ball and press it into a 9 x 13-inch baking dish, distributing it as evenly as possible and creating a slight rim (about ¼ inch) around the edges. Bake for 15 minutes, until it starts to look dry but not browned. Let cool for 10 to 15 minutes before filling.

5 Meanwhile, prepare the filling. Whisk together the eggs, sugar, orange zest and juice, lemon zest and juice, and flour until thoroughly combined and smooth. Pour the filling over the cooled crust and bake for about 35 minutes, until the filling is set and no longer jiggly. Let cool completely.

6 Combine the confectioners' sugar and *fleur de sel*, mixing to distribute the *fleur de sel* throughout the sugar. Sift enough of the sugar-salt mixture over the cooled bars to cover them with a thin layer of white dust. Cut into squares and serve. The bars will keep in an airtight container for up to 1 day at room temperature or up to 3 days in the refrigerator.

cakes and cupcakes

very vanilla cake

By "very vanilla," I do not mean boring. A dessert doesn't have to be fancy to be good. Sometimes in the interest of being more sophisticated, more creative, and more over-the-top, we forget about the delicious basics, like a freshly baked, fragrantly yummy vanilla cake. Loaded with vanilla flavor, it's lovely, inviting, and oh so good.

1 cup (2 sticks) unsalted butter, softened

1 cup granulated sugar

2 teaspoons pure vanilla extract

3 large eggs

2 cups all-purpose flour, sifted

2½ teaspoons baking powder

½ teaspoon fine sea salt

¼ cup milk

Vanilla Simple Syrup (page 66)

1 tablespoon Vanilla Sugar, for sprinkling (optional; page 66)

Grinder sea salt for sprinkling

1 Preheat the oven to 325°F. Line the bottom of an 8-inch square baking dish with parchment paper, and butter the sides of the dish.

2 Combine the butter and granulated sugar in the bowl of a stand mixer fitted with a paddle attachment and beat until light and creamy. Mix in the vanilla. Beat in the eggs one at a time, scraping down the sides of the bowl after each addition.

3 Sift together the flour, baking powder, and fine sea salt. Add half of the flour mixture to the batter and beat until combined, then add the milk and beat until combined. Add the remaining flour mixture, and mix until just combined. Pour the batter into the prepared dish and bake for about 1 hour, until the top of the cake is golden brown and a cake tester comes out clean.

4 Brush the top of the warm cake with Vanilla Simple Syrup and sprinkle with Vanilla Sugar, if desired, and a hint of grinder sea salt. Let the cake cool for at least 30 minutes before cutting. Serve warm or at room temperature. The cake will keep, covered, at room temperature for up to 2 days.

(continued)

vanilla simple syrup

MAKES 1 CUP

½ cup sugar
1 teaspoon pure vanilla extract
Pinch of fine sea salt
1 cup water

Combine the sugar, vanilla, salt, and water in a small saucepan over low heat and simmer, stirring occasionally, for 4 to 5 minutes, until the sugar is dissolved. Use immediately, or refrigerate in an airtight container for up to 2 days.

SWEET IDEAS!
* Serve with a side of fresh berries or Blackberry-Caramel Sauce (page 130).
* Frost with Snappy Butterscotch Icing (page 68) or Coconut Buttercream Frosting (page 71).

vanilla sugar

MAKES ½ CUP

½ cup sanding sugar
1 vanilla bean, split lengthwise

Combine the sugar and vanilla bean and store in an airtight container for at least 2 days before using.

dark chocolate fleur de sel cupcakes with snappy butterscotch icing

MAKES 12 TO 14 CUPCAKES

Oh, do I love cupcakes. They are absolutely the perfect treat. I might even be a little obsessed. I am constantly pitching food editors stories about cupcakes, just so I have an excuse to sample more. (I think they're on to me now.) I take my friend Carrie's three-year-old daughter, Caitlin, out for cupcakes—claiming it's because she loves them so much. (She does love them—after her first bite of a lemon cupcake on our last date, she looked up at me with a huge grin and exclaimed, "This is delicious!") While planning my wedding, the part I was most excited about (aside from marrying Will) was the cupcakes we decided to serve instead of a big wedding cake. There were three kinds, including a chocolate cupcake—sprinkled with *fleur de sel*, of course.

1 cup all-purpose flour
½ cup unsweetened cocoa powder
½ cup granulated sugar
½ cup packed light brown sugar
1 teaspoon baking soda
¼ teaspoon fine sea salt
5 tablespoons unsalted butter
3 tablespoons canola oil
⅓ cup water
1 large egg
¼ cup buttermilk
1½ teaspoons pure vanilla extract
Fleur de sel
Snappy Butterscotch Icing (page 68)

1 Preheat the oven to 350°F. Line a 12-cup muffin tin with cupcake liners.

2 Sift the flour, cocoa powder, granulated sugar, brown sugar, baking soda, and fine sea salt together into the bowl of a stand mixer fitted with a whisk attachment.

3 In a small saucepan, heat the butter, oil, and water over medium-low heat, stirring until the butter is completely melted and incorporated.

4 Whisk the butter mixture into the dry ingredients on low speed until thoroughly combined. Whisk in the egg, then whisk in the buttermilk and vanilla.

5 Fill the cupcake liners three-quarters full with batter and sprinkle a tiny bit of *fleur de sel* over the top of each. Bake for 22 to 24 minutes, until the tops of the cupcakes are set and spring back when you touch them and a cake tester comes out clean.

6 Let cool for 5 minutes in the pan, then transfer to a wire rack to cool completely. Ice with Snappy Butterscotch Icing. The cupcakes will keep, covered, at room temperature for up to 2 days.

(continued)

snappy butterscotch icing

MAKES ABOUT 1½ CUPS (ENOUGH TO ICE
12 REGULAR-SIZE CUPCAKES)

½ cup packed light brown sugar
1 cup heavy cream
2 tablespoons unsalted butter
1 teaspoon water
¼ teaspoon fine sea salt

1 Combine the sugar, cream, butter, water, and salt in a medium-size saucepan over medium-low heat and stir until the butter is melted and the sugar is completely dissolved, 3 to 5 minutes.

2 Turn the heat down to low and let simmer for 8 minutes without stirring, until the icing has thickened. Remove from the heat and let cool completely so the icing will thicken enough to spread. Refrigerate or freeze for 30 minutes to speed the thickening process, if you like. The icing can be stored in an airtight container in the refrigerator for up to 3 days.

SWEET IDEAS!
* For a double dose of chocolate, frost these cupcakes with Chocolate Frosting (page 74).
* Skip the icing altogether, sprinkle these with a tiny bit more *fleur de sel* immediately after they come out of the oven, and serve warm with a scoop of Butterscotch Ice Cream (page 120) on the side.

mini coconut cupcakes with coconut buttercream frosting

MAKES 36 TO 40 MINI CUPCAKES

If cupcakes are cute, mini cupcakes are over-the-top adorable. Even better if they taste insanely good and stay moist and delicious. With smaller cupcakes, there's an increased risk of dryness, but not with these sweet little things. The coconut milk and lower oven temperature keep the texture perfect, and the almond flavoring complements the coconut phenomenally well.

2 cups all-purpose flour
¾ teaspoon baking powder
½ teaspoon baking soda
½ teaspoon fine sea salt
1 cup (2 sticks) unsalted butter, softened
1 cup granulated sugar
¼ cup packed light brown sugar
3 large eggs
1 teaspoon pure vanilla extract
1 teaspoon pure almond extract
¾ cup coconut milk
½ cup unsweetened shredded coconut, plus more for sprinkling
Grinder sea salt
Coconut Buttercream Frosting (recipe follows)

1 Preheat the oven to 325°F. Line mini muffin tins with mini paper liners.

2 Sift the flour, baking powder, baking soda, and fine sea salt together in a medium-size bowl.

3 In the bowl of a stand mixer fitted with a paddle attachment, beat the butter, granulated sugar, and brown sugar together until light and fluffy, about 4 minutes. Add the eggs one at a time and beat on low speed to combine, scraping down the sides of the bowl after each addition. Add the vanilla and almond extracts and mix until well combined.

4 Add the dry ingredients alternately with the coconut milk in 3 increments, starting and ending with the dry ingredients and beating after each addition, until just combined. Stir in the coconut by hand.

5 Spoon the batter into the muffin cups, filling to just below the top of the liner. Sprinkle the batter with a very light dusting of grinder sea salt. Bake for about 15 minutes, until the tops of the cupcakes are light golden and a tester comes out clean.

6 Let cool in the pan for about 10 minutes, then transfer to a wire rack to cool completely. Frost with Coconut Buttercream Frosting and sprinkle with a pinch of shredded coconut. The cupcakes will keep, covered, at room temperature for up to 2 days.

coconut buttercream frosting

MAKES ABOUT 1¾ CUPS (ENOUGH TO FROST 36 TO 40 MINI CUPCAKES)

1 cup (2 sticks) unsalted butter, softened
3 cups confectioners' sugar
½ teaspoon pure vanilla extract
½ teaspoon pure almond extract
¼ teaspoon fine sea salt
2 tablespoons coconut milk, plus more if needed

1 Beat the butter with a hand mixer or electric mixer on medium-low speed until smooth and creamy.

2 Add the confectioners' sugar, vanilla extract, almond extract, and salt, and mix on low speed until the sugar is just incorporated. Increase the speed to medium and beat until smooth, about 1 minute.

3 Add the coconut milk and beat until light and fluffy, about 2 minutes, adding a little more coconut milk as needed if the frosting seems too dry. The frosting will keep in an airtight container in the refrigerator for up to 2 days.

SWEET IDEA!
If you're a fan of the coconut and chocolate combo, try frosting these cupcakes with Chocolate Frosting (page 74) before sprinkling on the shredded coconut.

peanut butter cupcakes with chocolate frosting

MAKES ABOUT 12 CUPCAKES

It's hard to go wrong with the peanut butter and chocolate combination. I know. I've tried just about all of them. One night, in desperation, I even stirred up a glob of creamy peanut butter with a little cocoa powder and ate it with a spoon. It did the trick! But I'll definitely take these cupcakes, with a peanut buttery cake and creamy chocolate frosting, over that concoction anytime.

1 cup all-purpose flour
1 teaspoon baking powder
½ teaspoon salt
6 tablespoons (¾ stick) unsalted butter, softened
¾ cup creamy peanut butter (regular, not natural)
½ cup packed light brown sugar
¼ cup granulated sugar
1 large egg
2 teaspoons pure vanilla extract
½ cup whole milk
Chocolate Frosting (page 74)
Fleur de sel or chopped salted peanuts for sprinkling
   (optional)

1 Preheat the oven to 350°F. Line a 12-cup muffin tin with cupcake liners.

2 Sift the flour, baking powder, and salt together into a medium-size bowl.

3 In the bowl of a stand mixer fitted with a paddle attachment, beat the butter, peanut butter, brown sugar, and granulated sugar together on medium speed until light-colored and creamy, about 1 minute.

4 Beat in the egg for 30 seconds. Scrape down the sides of the bowl, then mix in the vanilla and beat on medium speed for 1 minute. Scrape down the sides of the bowl again.

5 Add the flour mixture in 3 increments, alternating with the milk (which you'll add in 2 increments), beginning and ending with the flour mixture and beating after each addition. Mix until just combined.

6 Fill each cupcake liner three-quarters full with batter. Bake for about 20 minutes, until the tops of the cupcakes are golden and firm and a cake tester comes out clean. Let cool in the pan on a wire rack for 15 minutes, then transfer the cupcakes to a wire rack to cool completely before frosting. When cool, frost each cupcake with chocolate frosting. Sprinkle lightly with either *fleur de sel* or chopped salted peanuts, if desired. The frosted cupcakes will keep, covered, at room temperature for up to 2 days.

(continued)

chocolate frosting

MAKES ABOUT 1 CUP (ENOUGH TO FROST ABOUT
12 REGULAR-SIZE CUPCAKES)

4 ounces bittersweet chocolate, chopped
½ cup heavy cream
3 tablespoons unsalted butter
1 tablespoon light corn syrup
¼ teaspoon fine sea salt

1 Put the chocolate in a medium-size heatproof bowl and set aside.

2 Combine the cream, butter, corn syrup, and salt in a small saucepan and heat over medium heat until very hot but not boiling, about 4 minutes.

3 Quickly pour the hot cream mixture over the chopped chocolate. Let stand for 5 to 7 minutes to melt the chocolate, then whisk until smooth. Refrigerate for 30 minutes, then beat with an electric mixer until light and fluffy. The frosting will keep for up to 3 days, refrigerated, in an airtight container. Bring to room temperature before using.

SWEET IDEA!
Make these cupcakes fun and kid-friendly by omitting the sprinkling of *fleur de sel* on top of the frosting and topping them instead with crushed peanut butter cups or a few Reese's Pieces.

almond-orange torte

My friend Meg's birthday is in June, and I always try to celebrate it with her. It's one of my favorite beginning-of-summer rituals. Once I rented a little cottage near the beach in Rhode Island for part of the summer, so we had Meg's birthday there that year. A small group of us toasted the evening with Champagne and then enjoyed an incredible almond torte from my favorite Rhode Island bakery, Provender Fine Foods. I'm a little fuzzy on the details from later in the night (I know there was more Champagne), but everyone had a very good time. I now think very fondly of almond torte, which is an elegant cake for any occasion, especially a spring or summer birthday when the guest of honor doesn't want heaps of buttercream. This one has delicious citrus flavor, just enough saltiness, and an almondy, orangey glaze that brings the whole thing together.

1 cup whole unsalted almonds
½ cup (1 stick) unsalted butter, softened
¾ cup sugar
3 large eggs (1 whole and 2 separated)
2 tablespoons fresh orange juice
1 teaspoon pure almond extract
½ cup all-purpose flour
1 tablespoon orange zest
½ teaspoon fine sea salt
Almond-Orange Glaze (page 76)

1 Preheat the oven to 375°F. Generously butter a 9-inch round springform pan. Line the bottom of the pan with parchment paper, and butter and flour the parchment.

2 In a food processor or coffee grinder, grind the almonds to a fine powder. Set aside.

3 In the bowl of a stand mixer fitted with a paddle attachment, cream the butter on medium-high speed until light and fluffy. Add the sugar and beat until well combined.

4 Beat in the whole egg, then beat in the egg yolks one at a time. Scrape the sides of the bowl after adding each yolk. Add the orange juice and almond extract. Then, on low speed, mix in the ground almonds, flour, orange zest, and salt.

5 In a separate bowl, beat the egg whites with an electric hand mixer until stiff peaks form. Gently fold the egg whites into the batter.

6 Pour the batter into the springform pan and bake for about 25 minutes, until the top of the cake is light golden brown and a cake tester comes out clean. Let the cake cool for at least 30 minutes in the pan on a wire rack.

7 Pour the glaze over the torte, cut into wedges, and serve. The glazed torte will keep, covered, for up to 2 days at room temperature, or for up to 1 month in the freezer, wrapped tightly in 2 layers of plastic wrap.

(continued)

almond-orange glaze

MAKES ABOUT ½ CUP

1 cup confectioners' sugar
2 tablespoons fresh orange juice
½ teaspoon pure almond extract
½ teaspoon fine sea salt

Combine the confectioners' sugar, orange juice, almond extract, and salt in a small bowl and whisk until thoroughly combined.

SWEET IDEA!
If you don't want to glaze the torte, combine ¼ cup confectioners' sugar with ½ teaspoon *fleur de sel* and sift the sugar-salt mixture lightly over the top of the cooled torte.

kickass carrot cake with maple–cream cheese frosting

SERVES 10

Carrot cake hasn't always been a favorite of mine—I've been disappointed at weddings and birthday parties when a cake I thought was going to be chocolate turned out to be carrot. But carrot cake is the favorite of my husband, Will. So for a recent birthday I decided to come up with a kickass carrot cake in the salty-sweet vein. After many attempts (and a true immersion into the world of carrot cake so I could understand what makes it tick), I came up with this recipe. And oh, does it kick ass: rich, a little spicy, super-moist, and delicious. The cream cheese frosting used here, flavored with real maple syrup (don't use the fake stuff!), isn't as cloyingly sweet as many cream cheese frostings. Finally, I understand the love affair so many people have with carrot cake. Will gives it a big thumbs-up, too.

2 cups all-purpose flour

2 teaspoons baking soda

1½ teaspoons fine sea salt

2 teaspoons ground cinnamon

1 teaspoon ground ginger

2 cups sugar

1¼ cups canola oil

4 large eggs

3 cups peeled grated carrots

1 cup chopped toasted walnuts (page 13)

½ cup Snappy Butterscotch Sauce (optional; page 128)

Maple–Cream Cheese Frosting (page 78)

1 Preheat the oven to 350°F. Butter two 9-inch round cake pans and line the bottoms of the pans with parchment paper. Butter and flour the parchment paper.

2 Sift the flour, baking soda, salt, cinnamon, and ginger together into a medium-size bowl.

3 In the bowl of a stand mixer fitted with a whisk attachment, whisk together the sugar and oil until well blended. Whisk in the eggs, one at a time. Add the dry ingredients to the mixer bowl and stir until just blended. Fold in the carrots and walnuts.

4 Divide the batter between the cake pans and bake for 30 to 35 minutes, until a cake tester comes out clean.

5 Let the cakes cool in the pans for 20 minutes, then transfer them to wire racks to cool. Remove the parchment paper from the bottoms and let cool completely.

6 Brush each cake layer with warmed Snappy Butterscotch Sauce, if desired. Spread a generous layer of frosting on top of one cake layer, place the second layer on top of that, and spread the rest of the frosting all over the cake. Serve immediately, or cover and refrigerate for up to 2 days.

(continued)

maple–cream cheese frosting

MAKES ABOUT 2½ CUPS, ENOUGH TO FROST ONE
9-INCH LAYER CAKE

10 ounces cream cheese
6 tablespoons (¾ stick) unsalted butter, softened
3 cups confectioners' sugar
⅓ cup pure maple syrup
½ teaspoon fine sea salt

1 In the bowl of a stand mixer fitted with a paddle attachment or using an electric hand mixer, beat the cream cheese and butter together for about 2 minutes, until light and fluffy.

2 Add the confectioners' sugar and beat on low speed until well blended. Mix in the maple syrup, then mix in the sea salt.

SWEET IDEA!
For a little extra texture and visual appeal, sprinkle ¾ cup chopped toasted walnuts or pecans evenly over the top of the frosted cake and press them gently into the frosting to set.

Opposite: Cranberry Coffee Cake, page 80

cranberry **coffee cake**

MAKES ONE 8-INCH TUBE CAKE

My mom makes a coffee cake almost exactly like this every year on Christmas morning, and it's the best treat of the day. The years when I'm not home for the holidays and don't get to have this cake, it always feels like something is missing. The cake is so good that it's practically impossible to have just one piece.

2 cups all-purpose flour
1 teaspoon baking soda
1 teaspoon baking powder
½ teaspoon fine sea salt
½ cup (1 stick) unsalted butter, softened
1 cup sugar
2 large eggs
1 teaspoon pure almond extract
1 cup sour cream
2 cups whole-berry cranberry sauce
½ cup chopped toasted walnuts (page 13)
¼ teaspoon grinder sea salt
Almond-Sugar Glaze (recipe follows)

1 Preheat the oven to 350°F. Butter an 8-inch tube pan.

2 In a medium-size bowl, sift together the flour, baking soda, baking powder, and fine sea salt.

3 In the bowl of a stand mixer fitted with a paddle attachment, cream together the butter and sugar. Add the eggs one at a time, mixing well after each addition. Mix in the almond extract.

4 Add the dry ingredients (in 3 increments) alternately with the sour cream (in 2 increments), starting and ending with the dry ingredients, beating after each addition until just combined.

5 Pour half the batter into the prepared tube pan. Swirl half the cranberry sauce over the batter. Pour the remaining batter over the cranberry sauce and then swirl the remaining cranberry sauce over the batter. Toss the chopped walnuts with the grinder sea salt and sprinkle over the top of the cake.

6 Bake for 55 minutes, until golden brown on top. While the cake is baking, prepare the glaze. Let the cake cool in the pan for 5 minutes, then remove it from the pan to a wire rack and cool for another 10 minutes. Transfer the cake to a serving plate and drizzle the glaze all over the top. Serve warm or at room temperature. The cake will keep, covered, at room temperature for up to 2 days.

almond-sugar glaze

¾ cup confectioners' sugar
½ teaspoon pure almond extract
1 tablespoon warm water
¼ teaspoon fine sea salt

Mix together the sugar, almond extract, water, and salt in a small bowl until smooth.

SWEET IDEA!

To serve this for dessert, add a scoop of Almond Ice Cream (page 119) or Bittersweet Chocolate Ice Cream (page 117) on top of or beside each slice of warm cake.

lemon cake with lemon–brown sugar glaze

MAKES ONE 9-INCH LOAF CAKE

I have always adored lemon cake. When I was little I called it lemonade cake, and I always requested it for my birthday. My grandmother Doris baked her signature lemon cake in a loaf pan and topped it with a sweet lemon syrup, no frosting—so that's my vision of what a lemon cake should be. This one is super-lemony (I'm crushed when a so-called lemon cake is lacking in lemon flavor), and the glaze is made with brown sugar and a hint of sea salt.

½ cup (1 stick) unsalted butter, softened
¾ cup granulated sugar
¼ cup packed light brown sugar
1½ cups all-purpose flour
½ teaspoon baking powder
½ teaspoon baking soda
1 teaspoon fine sea salt
¼ cup fresh lemon juice
⅓ cup buttermilk
1 teaspoon pure vanilla extract
2 large eggs
¼ cup lemon zest (from 4 to 5 medium-size lemons)
Lemon–Brown Sugar Glaze (recipe follows)

1 Preheat the oven to 350°F. Butter and flour a 5 x 9-inch loaf pan.

2 In the bowl of a stand mixer fitted with a paddle attachment, cream together the butter, granulated sugar, and brown sugar for about 4 minutes, until light and fluffy.

3 While the mixer is doing its thing, in a medium-size bowl, sift together the flour, baking powder, baking soda, and salt. In a small bowl, combine the lemon juice, buttermilk, and vanilla.

4 When the creamed butter and sugar mixture is ready, beat in the eggs one at a time, then add the lemon zest. Add the dry ingredients to the mixer bowl in 3 increments, alternating with the buttermilk mixture (starting and ending with the dry ingredients) and beating after each addition, and mix until combined, scraping down the sides of the bowl several times.

5 Pour the batter into the prepared loaf pan, distributing it evenly and smoothing the top. Bake for 45 to 55 minutes, until the edges are light golden brown and a tester comes out clean. Let the cake cool in the pan for 15 minutes.

6 While the cake is cooling, prepare the glaze.

7 Turn the cake out of the pan onto a wire rack. Brush the top generously with the glaze, reserving any remaining glaze to drizzle over the cake just before serving. Let cool completely. The cake will keep, covered, at room temperature for up to 2 days.

lemon–brown sugar glaze

MAKES ENOUGH TO GLAZE ONE 9-INCH LOAF CAKE

¼ cup fresh lemon juice
¼ cup packed light brown sugar
⅛ teaspoon fine sea salt

Combine the lemon juice, brown sugar, and sea salt in a small saucepan. Cook, stirring, over low heat until the sugar is completely dissolved.

SWEET IDEAS!
❊ Serve with Strawberry–Brown Sugar Sauce (page 132) on the side.
❊ Make the cake even more citrusy by adding 1 tablespoon grated lime zest and 1 tablespoon grated orange zest along with the lemon zest.

puddings and more

caramel-butterscotch pudding

MAKES 6 SERVINGS

If you think butterscotch pudding is a boring dessert, please try this one. It's a zinger. Top it with Scotch-scented Brown Sugar Whipped Cream (page 137) for a dessert with a retro feel that's good enough for your most discriminating friends.

1 cup granulated sugar
¼ cup water
⅓ cup heavy cream
½ cup packed dark brown sugar
⅓ cup cornstarch
1 teaspoon fine sea salt
3 cups whole milk
4 large egg yolks
6 tablespoons (¾ stick) unsalted butter, cut into pieces
2 teaspoons pure vanilla extract

1 To make the caramel, combine the granulated sugar and water in a medium-size saucepan and stir over low heat until the sugar dissolves. Turn the heat up to high and boil, without stirring, until the mixture turns a deep golden brown color, 8 to 10 minutes. (Swirl the pan occasionally to promote even heating, and brush the sides of the pan with a wet pastry brush to prevent crystals from forming.)

2 Remove from the heat and add the cream carefully, because it will bubble up quite a bit. Stir until smooth, and reserve.

3 In another medium-size saucepan, combine the brown sugar, cornstarch, and salt, and whisk in the milk. Stir over medium-low heat until the mixture thickens and boils, 7 to 9 minutes. Remove from the heat and whisk in the caramel.

4 Whisk the egg yolks gently in a large bowl. To temper them, very slowly whisk in about ½ cup of the warm pudding mixture, being careful not to add too much too quickly or you'll cook the eggs and they'll get lumpy.

5 Once the yolks are tempered, whisk the yolk mixture into the pudding mixture and return the pudding to the stovetop, bringing it to a simmer over medium heat.

6 Whisk in the butter and vanilla. Remove from the heat and divide the pudding among 6 small bowls or ramekins. Refrigerate uncovered for 30 minutes, then cover the puddings with plastic wrap (directly on the pudding surface, to prevent a skin from forming on top) and refrigerate for at least another 3 hours or overnight. Serve within 1 day.

coconut rice pudding

Simple and creamy, this is pure comfort food with a slightly exotic twist in the form of coconut. Okay, maybe it's not that exotic, but it's really good. It's meant to be served warm, but I also like it cold out of the fridge the next day.

2 cups cooked jasmine rice
2 cups whole milk
1¾ cups coconut milk
½ cup unsweetened shredded coconut
⅓ cup sugar
1 teaspoon fine sea salt
1 teaspoon pure vanilla extract

1 Combine the rice, milk, coconut milk, coconut, sugar, and salt in a medium-size saucepan over medium-low heat and stir frequently, until thick, about 35 minutes.

2 Stir in the vanilla and simmer for 2 more minutes. Serve warm.

SWEET IDEAS!
* **Add 1 tablespoon grated lime zest to the saucepan and serve the pudding with fresh sliced mango.**
* **Add ½ teaspoon grated nutmeg to the rice mixture during cooking, and sprinkle each serving with a pinch of grated nutmeg.**

sticky toffee pudding
MAKES 10 SERVINGS

This is a British dessert that's called pudding, but it's really a gooey cake. I put it in this chapter out of respect for its title. (That's British of me, right?) It owes its gooeyness to the dates in the cake and to the decidedly gooey toffee sauce poured on top. Just try this dessert, I beg you. The toffee sauce alone is reason enough, and the cake rocks, too. I think dates are one of the most underrated treats out there. They are so good to eat straight as a snack you almost feel naughty (because they're so sticky, sweet, and pleasurable), but dates are actually pretty good for you (they contain fiber, potassium, and folate).

1½ cups pitted Medjool dates, coarsely chopped
1½ cups water
½ cup (1 stick) unsalted butter, softened
2 cups packed dark brown sugar
1 teaspoon pure vanilla extract
2 large eggs
3 cups all-purpose flour
1 teaspoon baking soda
1 teaspoon salt
Toffee Sauce (page 90)

1 Preheat the oven to 350°F. Butter an 8 x 12- or 9 x 13-inch baking dish.

2 Combine the dates and water in a medium-size saucepan and simmer over low heat, covered, for about 7 minutes, until the dates are soft. Remove the pan from the heat and let stand, covered, for 5 minutes. Drain well.

3 In the bowl of a stand mixer fitted with a paddle attachment, cream together the butter and brown sugar. Add the vanilla, and beat until light and fluffy. Beat in the eggs one at a time, scraping down the sides of the bowl after each addition.

4 In a medium-size bowl, combine the flour with the baking soda and salt. Add the flour mixture to the butter mixture and beat on low speed until combined. Fold in the softened dates. Transfer the batter to the prepared baking dish and bake for 45 minutes, until the pudding springs back when you touch it and a cake tester comes out clean.

5 While the cake is still very warm, use a fork to poke holes in the top. Pour about 1½ cups of warm toffee sauce over the pudding. Let the pudding cool in the pan on a wire rack for 20 to 30 minutes, until most of the sauce is absorbed. Cut into squares and serve from the pan, with the remaining toffee sauce on the side.

(continued)

toffee sauce

1 cup (2 sticks) unsalted butter
2 cups packed dark brown sugar
⅔ cup water
¼ teaspoon fine sea salt

Melt the butter in a medium-size saucepan over medium-low heat. Stir in the brown sugar, water, and salt. Turn the heat up to medium-high and bring to a boil; stir occasionally, cooking until the sauce is thickened slightly and reduced to about 2½ cups. Keep the sauce warm over very low heat until you're ready to use it.

SWEET IDEA!
Serve the warm cake with a scoop of vanilla ice cream or Almond Ice Cream (page 119) on the side.

chocolate chip bread pudding

I've never been a big fan of typical French toast—it always seems too sweet and too mushy to me. As desserts go, bread puddings are similar to French toast—they both start with bread that's been soaked in a creamy custard. The result is soft and delicious; I just don't want my bread pudding to be too soft. Made with ciabatta, this bread pudding has the perfect bite. Good-quality Italian or French bread would also work. This pudding is ridiculously good on its own, but it has been known to send people into throes of ecstasy when served with a dollop of Drunken Sauce (page 134). This is really easy to make, but for best results, start it a day in advance so the bread has time to absorb the custard.

12 ounces ciabatta, torn into 1- to 2-inch chunks
   (about 8 cups)
7 tablespoons unsalted butter, melted
1 cup semisweet or bittersweet chocolate chips
1¾ cups half-and-half
¼ cup granulated sugar
¼ cup plus 1 tablespoon packed dark brown sugar
4 large eggs
3 large egg yolks
2 tablespoons pure vanilla extract
½ teaspoon fine sea salt
Grinder sea salt

1 Generously butter a deep 9- or 10-inch round baking dish.

2 In a large bowl, toss the bread pieces with 6 tablespoons of the melted butter. Toss with the chocolate chips and place the mixture in the prepared baking dish.

3 In a large bowl, whisk together the half-and-half, granulated sugar, ¼ cup of the brown sugar, the eggs, egg yolks, vanilla, and fine sea salt. Pour the egg mixture over the bread, then press the bread down into the liquid so it absorbs more. Cover and refrigerate for at least 4 hours, or, preferably, overnight.

4 Preheat the oven to 350°F.

5 Remove the baking dish from the refrigerator and drizzle with the remaining 1 tablespoon melted butter, the remaining 1 tablespoon brown sugar, and 2 pinches of grinder sea salt. Place the baking dish in a larger baking pan, then carefully pour enough water into the larger pan to reach 1 to 2 inches up the side of the dish.

6 Bake for about 1 hour, or until the bread pudding has puffed up a bit and is golden brown on top. Serve immediately.

milk chocolate–peanut butter mousse

MAKES 6 SERVINGS

It doesn't get much more comforting than this. Featuring mostly milk chocolate (punctuated with a little dark chocolate) and peanut butter, this rich, easy-to-make mousse offers a creamy combination of the sweet-salty flavors everyone loves together—and a little of this goes a long way. Garnish the mousse with a bit of Milk Chocolate–Peanut Butter Crunch for a textural contrast.

½ cup creamy peanut butter (regular, not natural)
9 ounces milk chocolate, chopped
3 ounces bittersweet chocolate, chopped
½ teaspoon fine sea salt
¾ cup milk
1 cup heavy cream
Milk Chocolate–Peanut Butter Crunch for garnish
  (optional; recipe follows)

1 Combine the peanut butter, milk chocolate, bittersweet chocolate, and salt in a medium-size saucepan over medium-low heat and stir until the peanut butter and chocolate are melted and smooth. Transfer the chocolate–peanut butter mixture to a medium-size mixing bowl.

2 Heat the milk to scalding (the point at which small bubbles are forming around the edge of the pan but the milk is not yet boiling) in a small saucepan over medium heat. Whisk the hot milk into the chocolate–peanut butter mixture. Let cool to room temperature.

3 In a medium-size bowl, beat the heavy cream with an electric mixer on high speed until soft peaks form. Fold the whipped cream into the chocolate–peanut butter mixture until thoroughly combined and uniform in color. Refrigerate, covered, for at least 30 minutes and up to 1 day. Serve topped with the Milk Chocolate–Peanut Butter Crunch.

milk chocolate–peanut butter crunch

MAKES ABOUT 2¼ CUPS

¼ cup creamy peanut butter (regular, not natural)
2 ounces milk chocolate, chopped
2 cups cornflakes

1 Line a baking sheet with parchment paper.

2 Combine the peanut butter and chocolate in a small saucepan over medium-low heat and stir until the peanut butter and chocolate are melted and smooth. Stir in the cornflakes.

3 Spread the mixture on the baking sheet in a layer about ½ inch thick and refrigerate until firm, about 1 hour. Break the crunch into bite-size pieces and use it as a garnish for the mousse (or snack on it as is!). The crunch keeps in the refrigerator in an airtight container for up to 1 week.

maple crème brûlée

MAKES 6 SERVINGS

Don't be afraid of making crème brûlée. Maybe you're not afraid of it—I used to be, till I tried it and learned that it's not hard at all. You just need to give yourself enough time to let everything cool and set. Start this at least a couple of hours before you want to serve it, then caramelize the top (the fun part, which you can do with a kitchen blowtorch or under the broiler) at the last minute before serving. A dash of sea salt plays beautifully against the sweetness of the maple and the hard sugar crust. Be sure to use real maple syrup, not the imitation stuff.

3 cups heavy cream
1 cup pure maple syrup
5 large egg yolks
1 large egg
1 teaspoon pure vanilla extract
1 teaspoon sea salt
½ cup sugar
1 cup fresh seasonal berries of your choice, for garnish
  (optional)

1 Preheat the oven to 350°F.

2 In a medium-size saucepan, heat the cream and maple syrup over medium heat, stirring occasionally, until steam rises from the surface. Do not let it boil. Remove from the heat.

3 In a medium-size bowl, stir the egg yolks and the egg together to blend well. Stir the vanilla into the cream mixture, then slowly pour in the eggs in 3 increments, stirring gently between each increment. Place the saucepan in an ice-water bath for about 10 minutes to cool the custard. Stir gently once or twice to speed the cooling process.

4 Divide the custard among six 6-ounce ramekins. Place the ramekins in an ovenproof baking dish and carefully pour enough water into the dish to come halfway up the sides of the ramekins. Bake until the custard is firm, 45 to 50 minutes. Remove the ramekins from the baking dish and let them cool at room temperature for up to 2 hours. Once they've reached room temperature, you can refrigerate them for up to 8 hours.

5 When it's almost time to serve, preheat the broiler. Set the ramekins on a baking sheet and sprinkle each custard with some of the sea salt, then some of the sugar (sugar should be about ¼ inch thick on each ramekin, evenly distributed).

6 Place the ramekins under the broiler, close to the heat source. Remove from the heat when the tops are golden brown and hardened, 2 to 3 minutes.

7 Garnish with berries, if desired, and serve warm, or refrigerate for at least 10 minutes and up to 2 hours, then garnish with berries and serve cold.

fruits

berry berry shortcakes

In Westford, Massachusetts, where I grew up, there is a Strawberries & Art Festival every year in mid-June, held on the town common. The big draw is the strawberry shortcake, doled out in heaping portions with plenty of fresh whipped cream. When I was little, that was the only reason I wanted to go. Though I haven't attended the festival in years, strawberry shortcake is still one of my all-time faves. How can you go wrong? A simple shortcake split in two with fresh berries and whipped cream? All good. I especially love it with a mix of berries (when in season) and a touch of salt on top of the shortcakes, which makes them a little more savory and complements the sweet berries and cream. The Salted Shortcakes are also good with Roasted Summer Fruits (page 107) and a spoonful of Snappy Butterscotch Sauce (page 128).

3 cups fresh strawberries, hulled and quartered
3 cups fresh blueberries
¼ cup fresh orange juice
1 tablespoon sugar
Salted Shortcakes (recipe follows)
Brown Sugar Whipped Cream (page 137) or plain
   whipped cream

1 Combine the strawberries, blueberries, orange juice, and sugar in a medium-size bowl. Cover and refrigerate for at least 1 hour, until the berries have released some of their juices.

2 Split the shortcakes in half. Spoon a generous amount of berries on the bottom half of each, top with a dollop of whipped cream, and place the top half of each shortcake just slightly askew on top of that. Serve immediately.

salted shortcakes

MAKES EIGHT 3-INCH SHORTCAKES

3 cups all-purpose flour
¼ cup plus 1 teaspoon sugar
1 tablespoon baking soda
½ teaspoon fine sea salt
¾ cup (1½ sticks) cold unsalted butter, cut into small pieces
2 tablespoons grated orange zest
¾ cup buttermilk
2 tablespoons heavy cream
Grinder sea salt for sprinkling

1 Preheat the oven to 350°F.

2 Combine the flour, ¼ cup of the sugar, the baking soda, and the fine sea salt in the bowl of a stand mixer fitted with a paddle attachment. Mix on low speed for a few seconds. Add the cold butter pieces and mix on low just until the dough has a sandy, crumbly consistency.

3 Mix in the orange zest and then the buttermilk by hand until the dough is just moistened. Don't overmix. Transfer the dough to a clean surface and roll it out to about ½ inch thick. Cut it into eight 3-inch circles and arrange them on a baking sheet.

4 Brush the top of each circle with the cream and then sprinkle with the remaining 1 teaspoon sugar and a quick grind of sea salt.

5 Bake for 20 to 25 minutes, rotating the pan after 10 to 12 minutes, until the shortcakes are golden. Let cool for 20 to 30 minutes, then split in half horizontally. These are best served the day they are made.

cornmeal peach crisp

MAKES 8 SERVINGS

This crisp is inspired by Native American cooking, which features cornmeal and pine nuts in many delicious ways. Here those ingredients lend wonderful texture and flavor to the buttery, slightly salty topping of a homey dessert. Make this when peaches are in season locally—fresh, organic peaches make all the difference (mealy, flavorless, out-of-season supermarket peaches won't do). Serve this with vanilla ice cream or Almond Ice Cream (page 119).

7 to 8 cups peeled and sliced peaches
2 tablespoons fresh lemon juice
1 cup granulated sugar
½ cup packed light brown sugar
1¼ cups all-purpose flour
1 cup yellow cornmeal
1 teaspoon fine sea salt
¾ cup (1½ sticks) cold unsalted butter, cut into small pieces
½ cup toasted pine nuts (page 13)

1 Preheat the oven to 350°F.

2 Toss the peaches with the lemon juice in a medium-size bowl. In a small bowl, combine ½ cup of the granulated sugar, the brown sugar, and ¼ cup of the flour. Add the sugar mixture to the peaches and mix well. Pour the peach mixture into a 9-inch square baking dish.

3 To make the topping, in the bowl of a stand mixer fitted with a paddle attachment, combine the remaining 1 cup flour, the cornmeal, the remaining ½ cup granulated sugar, and the salt, and mix quickly to combine. Add the butter and mix on low speed until the topping is coarsely crumbly. Stir in the pine nuts.

4 Distribute the topping evenly over the peaches and bake until the juices are bubbly and the peaches are tender, 40 to 50 minutes. Serve warm.

brown sugar apple crisp

MAKES 6 TO 8 SERVINGS

If you're ever looking for a dessert that's easy to throw together, and you want something that's a guaranteed crowd-pleaser, make a fruit crisp. Warm, gooey fruits paired with buttery, cinnamony, brown-sugary topping never miss. Add a dash of salt to the topping, as in this recipe, and serve the crisp warm with ice cream (vanilla is perfect, of course; you could also try it with the Almond Ice Cream on page 119 or the Butterscotch Ice Cream on page 120), and you're in for a treat.

4 pounds apples (preferably a mix of firm varieties, such as Granny Smith, Macoun, and Jonagold), peeled, cored, and cut into 1-inch wedges

1 teaspoon pure vanilla extract

1 teaspoon pure almond extract

1 cup plus 1 tablespoon all-purpose flour

1¼ cups packed light brown sugar

3 teaspoons ground cinnamon

1 cup old-fashioned or quick-cooking rolled oats (not instant)

½ teaspoon ground nutmeg

¾ cup (1½ sticks) cold unsalted butter, cut into small pieces

1 teaspoon fine sea salt

Grinder sea salt

1 Preheat the oven to 350°F.

2 In a large bowl, toss the apple wedges with the extracts. Add 1 tablespoon of the flour, ¼ cup of the brown sugar, and 1 teaspoon of the cinnamon. Toss to combine, and set aside.

3 To make the topping, in the bowl of a stand mixer fitted with a paddle attachment, combine the remaining 1 cup flour, the remaining 1 cup brown sugar, the oats, the remaining 2 teaspoons cinnamon, the nutmeg, butter, and fine sea salt. Mix on low speed until coarsely crumbly.

4 Pour the apples into a 9-inch square or a 7 x 11-inch baking dish. Distribute the topping evenly over the apples. Sprinkle a few grinds of sea salt over the topping and bake for 50 minutes to 1 hour, or until the topping is golden brown and crisp and the juices are bubbling. Let cool for 5 minutes and serve warm.

> SWEET IDEAS!
> * In the summer, replace the apples with a mixture of peaches and blueberries or nectarines and raspberries.
> * Add 1 cup fresh or frozen cranberries plus ¼ cup granulated sugar to the apple mixture in Step 2.

individual blueberry-nectarine crumbles

MAKES 8 SERVINGS

In my opinion, when summer fruits are in season there's no reason to make any dessert other than a fruit dessert. It's the New Englander in me—where I live, these fruits are so fabulous and so fleeting that it feels like a crime not to take advantage of them. Serve these crumbles warm, with a dollop of ice cream, of course.

2 cups fresh blueberries

2 cups chopped nectarines

½ cup all-purpose flour

3 tablespoons granulated sugar

1 teaspoon pure almond extract (optional)

½ cup packed light brown sugar

½ cup old-fashioned rolled oats (not quick-cooking or instant)

½ cup pecans, chopped

½ teaspoon fine sea salt

¼ cup (½ stick) cold unsalted butter

1 Preheat the oven to 350°F.

2 Toss the blueberries and nectarines with 1 tablespoon of the flour, the granulated sugar, and the almond extract, if desired. Divide the fruits among eight 6-ounce ramekins.

3 Combine the brown sugar, the remaining 7 tablespoons flour, the oats, pecans, and salt in a medium-size bowl and mix well. Cut in the butter with a pastry blender or a fork until the butter is evenly distributed and in pieces about the size of small currants.

4 Sprinkle the oat mixture over the fruits, dividing it evenly among the ramekins. Bake until the fruit is bubbly and the topping is golden brown, about 20 minutes. Let cool slightly, then serve.

SWEET IDEA!
Replace the blueberries and nectarines with 4 cups of another pair of summer fruits that are in season at the same time, such as fresh figs and raspberries, which overlap fleetingly in many areas.

cherry johnnycake cobbler

MAKES 8 SERVINGS

I love fruit desserts that don't require fussing over a pie crust. For this cobbler, however, I do suggest fussing over the task of pitting fresh cherries instead of using frozen, if possible. The topping has a little additional twist besides the salt: cornmeal, which gives it great texture and reminds me of johnnycake, a rustic staple of early New England cooking that is now most strongly associated with Rhode Island. Rhode Islanders are proud of their food traditions—if you're there and you see johnnycakes (or "stuffies"—a description of which doesn't belong in a dessert cookbook) on a menu, always order them. Serve this with a scoop of ice cream or a dollop of whipped cream.

1 cup plus 2 tablespoons sugar

2 tablespoons cornstarch

8 cups fresh or frozen pitted cherries

1 tablespoon plus 1 teaspoon pure vanilla extract

1 teaspoon lemon zest

1¼ teaspoons fine sea salt

1 cup all-purpose flour

3 tablespoons yellow cornmeal

1½ teaspoons baking powder

5 tablespoons cold unsalted butter, cut into pieces

½ cup whole milk

1 Preheat the oven to 375°F.

2 In a large heavy saucepan, whisk together 1 cup of the sugar and the cornstarch. Add the cherries, 1 tablespoon of the vanilla, the lemon zest, and ¼ teaspoon of the salt and bring to a boil over medium-high heat, stirring occasionally. Turn the heat down to medium-low and let simmer for about 2 minutes, until slightly thickened. Pour the cherries into a shallow 2-quart baking dish.

3 In the bowl of a stand mixer fitted with a paddle attachment, combine the flour, cornmeal, the remaining 2 tablespoons sugar, the baking powder, the remaining 1 teaspoon salt, and the butter and mix on low speed until the mixture resembles coarse meal.

4 Add the milk and the remaining 1 teaspoon vanilla and mix on low speed just until a dough forms.

5 Drop the dough in clumps onto the cherries, distributing the dough evenly over the cherries but not covering them completely. Bake for 35 to 45 minutes, until the johnnycake topping is golden brown and cooked through. Let cool for 10 minutes before serving warm.

walnut-crusted lemon tart

MAKES ONE 9-INCH TART

This recipe, with some minor tweaking, comes from my friend and confidante Tina Miller, an incredible, instinctive chef and the coauthor on my first cookbook, *Vineyard Harvest: A Year of Good Food on Martha's Vineyard* (Broadway Books, 2005). The tart features a brilliant, flour-free crust, and the flavor of the buttery, slightly salty walnuts is delicious with the zippy lemon filling. Be sure not to skimp on the fresh lemon juice or zest here!

3 cups walnuts

1¼ cups sugar

¾ teaspoon fine sea salt

¼ cup (½ stick) unsalted butter, melted, plus 6
    tablespoons (¾ stick) unsalted butter, cut into 6 pieces

2 large eggs

4 large egg yolks

3 tablespoons grated lemon zest

¾ cup fresh lemon juice

1 Preheat the oven to 350°F.

2 Combine the walnuts, ¼ cup of the sugar, and ½ teaspoon of the salt in a food processor and pulse until the walnuts are evenly ground, but not ground into a fine dust.

3 Scrape the walnut mixture into a large bowl. Add the melted butter and mix well. Press the mixture evenly into a 9-inch tart pan with a removable bottom. Bake for about 25 minutes, until the crust is slightly golden.

4 Turn the oven temperature down to 325°F.

5 Whisk the eggs and yolks together in a medium-size bowl. Add the remaining 1 cup sugar, the zest, and the remaining ¼ teaspoon salt and whisk for about 1 minute. Pour into a medium-size saucepan and cook over low heat, whisking constantly.

6 Add the lemon juice in 3 increments, whisking after each addition until the mixture thickens. When the mixture has thickened after the last addition of lemon juice, turn the heat down to very low and add the remaining butter 1 piece at a time, whisking it in completely after each addition.

7 While the mixture is still warm, pour it through a fine-mesh strainer into the prepared crust. Bake for about 10 minutes, until the filling is set. Chill the tart for at least 1 hour (or cover and refrigerate for up to 2 days) before serving.

SWEET IDEA!
Serve the tart with fresh berries or a dollop of Strawberry–Brown Sugar Sauce (page 132) or Blackberry-Caramel Sauce (page 130) on the side.

fig and ricotta **pizza**

My ideal meal involves pizza—really good pizza—and Champagne. Obviously, I also love sweets, so the idea of a sophisticated dessert pizza is heavenly to me. Figs are one of my favorite fruits, and when they are in season I use them in everything. They are phenomenal on savory pizza, especially when paired with a salty cured ham, and they taste delicious on this particular dessert pizza with creamy ricotta and a drizzle of melted chocolate. The dough here is simple—no yeast or rising required. It works for savory pizzas, too, so it's a really versatile staple to add to your repertoire. If you don't want to make your own pizza dough, stop by your favorite pizza shop and ask if they sell unbaked pizza dough. Most do, and it will be fresher than what you'd find in the supermarket.

Milk and Butter Pizza Dough (page 106)
¾ cup ricotta cheese
2 pints fresh figs, stems removed and sliced horizontally
  into rounds
2 tablespoons unsalted butter, melted
1 teaspoon *fleur de sel*
2 ounces bittersweet chocolate, melted

SWEET IDEAS!
* **Replace the figs with sliced fresh strawberries.**
* **Replace the figs with sliced peaches and replace the bittersweet chocolate with white chocolate.**

1 Preheat the oven to 450°F.

2 Spread the ricotta over the prepared dough, and arrange the fig slices on top of the ricotta (in a neat, pretty pattern, if you like).

3 Brush the melted butter over the figs and the edge of the crust. Sprinkle the figs and the crust very lightly with *fleur de sel*. Bake for about 20 minutes, until the crust is golden brown. Drizzle with lines of melted chocolate. Let cool for 2 to 3 minutes so the chocolate sets a bit, then serve immediately.

(continued)

milk and butter pizza dough

2¾ cups all-purpose flour, plus more for rolling
¾ cup whole milk
5 tablespoons unsalted butter, softened
1 teaspoon baking powder
1½ teaspoons fine sea salt

1 Combine the flour, milk, butter, baking powder, and salt in a large bowl and stir with a fork until a soft dough comes together. Shape the dough into a ball.

2 On a lightly floured surface, roll out the dough to a ⅛-inch-thick circle about 12 inches in diameter. While rolling, flip the dough occasionally so you're rolling it on both sides. It should be slightly thicker toward the edges. (You can also shape this dough by hand, but I find it easier to use a rolling pin.)

3 When it's rolled out to the desired size and thickness, transfer it to a baking sheet and form a little rim at the edge. Add toppings and bake as directed above. The dough can be made ahead, shaped into a ball, and refrigerated for up to 1 day or frozen for up to 2 weeks, tightly wrapped in plastic wrap. Defrost at room temperature for 3 to 4 hours if frozen, and let the dough come to room temperature before rolling.

roasted summer fruits

MAKES 8 SERVINGS

When the fruits of summer (peaches, nectarines, plums, raspberries) are in season, you don't need to do anything to them if you want a delicious treat. But it can be fun to play around with them just a bit. One of my favorite simple things to make for dinner is roasted seasonal vegetables—just toss whatever's fresh with a little oil, salt, and pepper and roast them in the oven. Why not do something similar with fruit? The result is warm, luscious, and simply good. The measurements and specific fruits listed here are just guidelines—feel free to use whatever looks good at your local farm stand or farmers' market. Serve the roasted fruit with ice cream, Brown Sugar Whipped Cream (page 137), or Lemon Cake (page 82).

4 nectarines, pitted and cut into sixths
4 peaches, pitted and cut into sixths
4 plums, pitted and quartered
1 tablespoon olive oil
1 tablespoon fresh orange juice
¼ cup sugar
½ teaspoon fine sea salt
1 pint fresh raspberries

1 Preheat the oven to 450°F.

2 Toss the nectarines, peaches, and plums with the olive oil, orange juice, sugar, and salt. Pour the fruits into a large baking dish and evenly distribute the raspberries on top.

3 Bake for about 25 minutes, until the fruits are tender and juicy. Serve warm.

oatmeal-crusted banana tart

I love to sprinkle a little salt on bananas and drizzle them with honey. This tart is a mouthwatering dessert version of that treat, all in a fantastic crust that reminds me of an oatmeal cookie. There are a few separate components to this dish, so it may seem complicated, but they are all really easy. And you can make the prebaked crust a day in advance if you like. The caramelized bananas are also tasty on their own or spooned over ice cream.

Caramelized Bananas (recipe follows)
¾ cup heavy cream
¾ cup sugar
Pinch of fine sea salt
Oatmeal Crust (recipe follows)
2 tablespoons light-flavored honey, slightly warmed
Fleur de sel

1 Preheat the oven to 350°F. Put the caramelized bananas in a large bowl.

2 Combine the cream, sugar, and salt in a small saucepan over medium heat and stir until the sugar dissolves and the cream just comes to a boil, 3 to 4 minutes. Pour the cream mixture over the bananas, and fold gently together.

3 Transfer the filling into the prebaked crust, evenly distributing the bananas, and bake for about 25 minutes, until the filling is bubbling. Let cool in the pan on a wire rack for 10 minutes, then push up from the bottom of the tart pan to release the tart from the sides of the pan. Let cool completely.

4 Drizzle the top of the tart with the honey and sprinkle with just a hint of *fleur de sel*. Serve immediately.

caramelized bananas

3 tablespoons unsalted butter
3 ripe but firm bananas, peeled and sliced into
   ½-inch-thick rounds
¼ cup packed light brown sugar
1 teaspoon fine sea salt

1 Melt the butter in a large skillet over medium heat, then add the bananas to the skillet in a single layer. Sprinkle the bananas with the brown sugar and salt.

2 Raise the heat to medium-high and cook the bananas for 3 to 4 minutes, turning them once about halfway through, until the sugar is caramelized.

oatmeal crust

MAKES ONE 9-INCH CRUST

1 cup (2 sticks) unsalted butter, at room temperature
½ cup packed light brown sugar
2 cups old-fashioned or quick-cooking rolled oats
  (not instant)
1 cup all-purpose flour
1 teaspoon fine sea salt

1 Preheat the oven to 350°F.

2 In the bowl of a stand mixer fitted with a paddle attachment, cream the butter and sugar together. Add the oats, flour, and salt and mix until just combined.

3 Cover the bowl with plastic wrap and refrigerate until the dough is firm, at least 30 minutes. Without overhandling the dough, shape it into a flat disk.

4 Press the dough evenly into a 10-inch tart pan with a removable bottom, being sure to press it into the sides and corners so there's no space between the pan and the dough. The dough should be uniformly thick on the bottom and sides of the pan. Trim off any excess dough from the edges.

5 Refrigerate for at least 30 minutes (or cover and refrigerate for up to 2 days). Butter one side of a sheet of aluminum foil and place it on top of the crust, butter side down. Top the foil with pie weights or dried beans. Bake for 10 minutes, then remove the weights and the foil and bake for another 3 minutes. The crust is now ready to use.

honey-tangerine caramel truffle tartlets

MAKES TEN 3½-INCH TARTLETS OR TWO 8-INCH TARTS

This recipe comes from my friend Joanne Chang, an amazing baker and the owner of Flour bakery in Boston. She and Flour's head pastry chef, Nicole Rhode, took a chocolate-making class several years ago, just to brush up on their skills. One of the recipes they learned was for a tangerine-caramel truffle, but since Flour doesn't generally sell truffles, Nicole adapted it into this honey-tangerine caramel tart topped with a thin layer of chocolate truffle and sprinkled with *fleur de sel*. This is a time-consuming recipe, but it's not difficult—and it's a showstopper.

PÂTE SUCRÉE (TART CRUST DOUGH)
½ cup plus 2 tablespoons (1¼ sticks) unsalted butter, softened
⅓ cup sugar
¼ teaspoon fine sea salt
1½ cups all-purpose flour
1 large egg yolk
2 tablespoons whole milk

CARAMEL
1 vanilla bean
1 cup heavy cream
½ cup plus 1½ tablespoons honey
¾ cup sugar
1½ tablespoons unsalted butter
¼ teaspoon fine sea salt
1 tablespoon tangerine zest

CHOCOLATE TRUFFLE
6 tablespoons heavy cream
¼ cup milk
3½ ounces bittersweet chocolate, chopped
1 large egg yolk
1 tablespoon unsalted butter
½ teaspoon fine sea salt

½ teaspoon *fleur de sel*

1 To make the *pâte sucrée*, in the bowl of a stand mixer fitted with a paddle attachment cream together the butter and sugar for 3 to 4 minutes. Mix in the salt. Add the flour and mix on low speed until just combined, scraping down the sides of the bowl several times. Add the egg yolk and milk and mix on low until the dough just comes together.

2 Turn out the dough onto a piece of plastic wrap and wrap the dough completely, pressing it down into a flat disk. Refrigerate the dough for at least 4 hours or overnight. (Note: The dough may be made up to this point and frozen for up to 1 month, wrapped tightly in 2 layers of plastic wrap and a layer of aluminum foil. Let it defrost in the refrigerator overnight before using.)

3 Use a rolling pin to roll out the chilled dough carefully between 2 sheets of parchment paper, until it is about ⅛ inch thick. Cut the dough into rounds slightly larger than your tartlet pans, and line the pans with the dough. Work quickly; this dough softens easily, which makes it difficult to work with. Refrigerate the tartlet shells for at least 1 hour to let the dough firm up and set.

4 Preheat the oven to 350°F. Bake the tartlet crusts until golden brown, 20 to 30 minutes. Let cool to room temperature before filling them.

5 To make the caramel, scrape the vanilla bean seeds into a small saucepan and add the scraped pod and the cream. Heat the mixture gently, over very low heat, for 10 minutes. Set the cream aside, keeping it warm, and remove the vanilla pod.

6 Combine the honey and sugar in a heavy medium-size pot. Cook the mixture until the temperature reaches 340°F on a candy thermometer, swirling the pan occasionally so the mixture heats evenly. Immediately add the warm vanilla cream while whisking gently. The caramel will bubble and steam vigorously, so be careful. Whisk in the butter, salt, and zest. Pour the caramel into the baked tartlet shells and let set at room temperature for approximately 30 minutes. Preheat the oven to 350°F.

7 To make the chocolate truffle, heat the cream and milk together in a medium-size pot until scalded (tiny bubbles will form on the surface; do not let it boil).

8 Put the chopped chocolate into a medium-size bowl, pour the cream and milk mixture over the chocolate, and whisk until melted. Whisk in the egg yolk and butter. Add the sea salt, and strain the mixture through a fine-mesh strainer.

9 Pour the chocolate truffle over the caramel-filled tartlets, distributing evenly. Bake for 6 minutes, then let set at room temperature for 1 hour. Sprinkle each tartlet with *fleur de sel* and serve.

ice creams
and sorbets

nantucket sea salt ice cream

MAKES ABOUT 1 QUART

No, you don't need to harvest your own salt from the waters around Nantucket to make this dessert. This recipe comes from my favorite restaurant on Nantucket, American Seasons (which also happens to be a favorite of certain celebrities who frequent the island, but owners Michael and Orla LaScola don't give up names). Seasons' pastry chef, Natasha Misanko, makes desserts that always bring more than just sweetness to the plate. She serves this simple, creamy ice cream with her pecan tart or with her fig and chocolate tart. Try it straight up, in between two Chocolate Oatmeal Cookies (page 45), or topped with Blackberry-Caramel Sauce (page 130).

2 cups heavy cream
1 cup half-and-half
¾ cup sugar
1 cup (10 to 12 large) egg yolks
1½ teaspoons coarse gray sea salt

1 Combine the cream, half-and-half, and sugar in a large heavy-bottomed saucepan over medium-high heat. Bring the mixture to a softly rolling boil and remove it from the heat.

2 Beat the egg yolks in a large bowl. Very slowly, add the heated cream mixture to the yolks (don't add it too quickly or you'll cook the yolks), whisking gently until thoroughly combined. Return the mixture to the saucepan and cook over medium heat until the mixture registers at least 160°F on an instant-read thermometer and is thick enough to coat the back of a spoon, 6 to 8 minutes. Cool completely in the refrigerator, at least 2 hours.

3 Process in an ice cream maker according to the manufacturer's instructions. About 2 minutes before the ice cream maker is done spinning, add the sea salt in a slow stream so it gets worked through the ice cream in a ribbon, not evenly distributed throughout, so you get a variety of texture and hits of saltiness against pure creaminess. (Using gray sea salt or another colored sea salt helps you see this ribbon and ensure that the salt isn't overly mixed in.) Serve immediately, or transfer to a container and return to the freezer for a firmer ice cream.

salted caramel ice cream

MAKES ABOUT 1 QUART

Bring together the concepts of salted caramel and home-made ice cream, and the result is one of my favorite treats ever. My favorite salted caramel ice cream comes from Bi-Rite Creamery & Bakeshop in the Mission neighborhood of San Francisco (as far as I'm concerned, the perfect gourmet night out includes dinner at Pizzeria Delfina and then a cone at Bi-Rite—please try that itinerary next time you're in SF), and this fairly easy version is just as addictive.

1¼ cups sugar
1 tablespoon light corn syrup
1 tablespoon water
2 cups heavy cream
2 cups whole milk
8 large egg yolks
1 teaspoon *fleur de sel*

1 Combine ¾ cup of the sugar, the corn syrup, and the water in a medium-size heavy saucepan and cook over medium-high heat without stirring—swirling the pan occasionally to help the sugar cook evenly—until it registers 340°F on a candy thermometer, about 7 minutes.

2 Turn the heat down to medium-low and carefully add the cream (it will bubble up quite a bit), and then slowly and carefully add the milk. The mixture will harden at this point. Turn the heat back up to medium-high and bring the mixture to a boil, then turn the heat back down to medium-low and let simmer, stirring until the caramel is dissolved.

3 In a separate bowl, combine the egg yolks with the remaining ½ cup sugar and the *fleur de sel*. Whisk until the sugar and salt are thoroughly incorporated. Whisk about 2 tablespoons of the hot caramel mixture into the yolk mixture to temper the eggs, then repeat with another 2 tablespoons of the caramel.

4 Pour the tempered egg mixture into the pan with the rest of the caramel and whisk to combine. Cook over medium-low heat until the mixture is thick enough to coat the back of a spoon (about 180°F on a candy thermometer—do not boil). Strain the mixture through a fine-mesh strainer into a metal bowl and refrigerate for at least 8 hours and up to overnight, covering it with plastic wrap after 1 hour of chilling.

5 Pour the mixture into the bowl of your ice cream maker and process according to the manufacturer's instructions. Transfer to a container and return to the freezer for at least 1 hour before serving.

bittersweet chocolate ice cream

MAKES ABOUT 1 QUART

I rarely order chocolate ice cream because it's so often a letdown, tasting more like sugar than actual chocolate. Not this one! Loaded with rich, bittersweet chocolate and sweetened with relatively little sugar (brown sugar, at that), it's intense and simple. The chocolate flavor is heightened even more by a hint of *fleur de sel* mixed in about halfway through the churning process. This isn't the first time I've said this, but it's key here: Use excellent chocolate. You will taste it!

2 cups heavy cream

1 cup whole milk

9 ounces bittersweet chocolate (around 60 percent cacao), chopped

½ cup packed light brown sugar

½ teaspoon *fleur de sel*

1 Heat the cream and milk together in a medium-size saucepan over medium heat until bubbling around the edges, but not boiling.

2 Place the chocolate in a medium-size heatproof bowl. Pour the hot cream mixture over the chocolate and let stand for 5 minutes to melt the chocolate. When the chocolate is melted, whisk the chocolate and cream mixture together until smooth. Whisk in the brown sugar until completely dissolved. Whisk in the *fleur de sel*. Refrigerate the chocolate mixture for at least 2 hours.

3 Pour the mixture into the bowl of your ice cream maker and process according to the manufacturer's instructions. Serve immediately, or transfer to a container and return to the freezer for a firmer ice cream.

> SWEET IDEA!
>
> For a simple but sophisticated presentation, drizzle 1 scoop of Bittersweet Chocolate Ice Cream with about 1 tablespoon of extra virgin olive oil and sprinkle the olive oil with a pinch or two of *fleur de sel*.

peanut butter ice cream

MAKES ABOUT 3 CUPS

If you love ice cream but do not have an ice cream maker, go get one. It will change your life. Making ice cream is so much fun, and—as this recipe demonstrates—so easy. My husband, Will, was a little skeptical about our need for an ice cream maker until he tasted this, one of the first ice cream recipes I came up with and tested. I gave him a little bite and he wanted more. So I dished some up and was about to top it with some Salted Milk Chocolate Sauce (page 126) when he stopped me and said, "No! I don't want anything to interfere with the ice cream!" He and his friend Bob polished off the entire rich, creamy batch in about 10 minutes. Peanut butter is perhaps the quintessential flavor for a salty sweet, and the brown sugar gives this a more interesting flavor than granulated sugar.

1 cup heavy cream
1 cup whole milk
½ cup packed light brown sugar
½ cup creamy peanut butter (regular, not natural)
1 teaspoon fine sea salt

1 Combine the cream, milk, sugar, and peanut butter in a medium-size bowl and whisk until the sugar is dissolved and the peanut butter is well incorporated. Whisk in the salt.

2 Chill the mixture in the freezer for 10 minutes. Pour the mixture into the bowl of your ice cream maker and process according to the manufacturer's instructions. Serve immediately, or transfer to a container and return to the freezer for a firmer ice cream.

almond ice cream

MAKES ABOUT 3 1/2 CUPS

By this point in the book you may have noticed my infatuation with anything almond flavored. So of course I wanted to include an almond ice cream. I played around with many versions, most of which started with an egg custard base. But I thought the flavor of the custard always interfered with the delicate almond flavor. And I don't want anything getting in the way of that! So I kept it very, very simple, and the result is fresh and delicious. Try this with fresh berries or with apple pie or apple crisp.

1 cup whole milk
1/2 cup packed light brown sugar
2 cups heavy cream
2 teaspoons pure almond extract
1/2 teaspoon fine sea salt
1/2 cup chopped almonds

1 In a large bowl, whisk together the milk and brown sugar until the sugar is dissolved. Whisk in the cream, almond extract, and salt.

2 Chill the mixture in the freezer for 10 minutes. Pour the mixture into the bowl of your ice cream maker and process according to the manufacturer's instructions.

3 About 1 minute before the ice cream maker is done, pour in the chopped almonds. Serve immediately (the ice cream will be fairly soft at this point), or transfer to a container and return to the freezer for a firmer ice cream.

butterscotch ice cream

MAKES ABOUT 1 QUART

I love the buttery, brown-sugary flavor of butterscotch sauce on just about any dessert, especially ice cream. So I thought it would be a good idea to combine those two things into one rich and delicious treat. And it turns out that it *is* a good idea. This ice cream is great on its own, with hot fudge sauce drizzled over it, or served on top of a fruit crisp.

½ cup packed light brown sugar
2½ cups heavy cream
2 tablespoons unsalted butter
½ teaspoon fine sea salt
1 cup whole milk

1 To make the butterscotch, combine the brown sugar, ½ cup of the cream, the butter, and salt in a small saucepan. Stir over low heat until the sugar is completely dissolved and the butter is completely melted. Raise the heat to medium and bring the mixture to a boil without stirring at all; boil for about 3 minutes. Watch it carefully to make sure it doesn't boil over. Let the butterscotch cool in the refrigerator for at least 2 hours or overnight.

2 In a large bowl, whisk together the milk, the remaining 2 cups cream, and the butterscotch until the butterscotch is dissolved. Chill the mixture in the freezer for 10 minutes. Pour the mixture into the bowl of your ice cream maker and process according to the manufacturer's instructions. Serve immediately (the ice cream will be fairly soft at this point), or transfer to a container and return to the freezer for a firmer ice cream.

coconut sorbet

This sorbet is an ideal after-dinner dessert—it's light and refreshing, but with enough richness and flavor to feel a little decadent. Top it with toasted shredded coconut or a light sprinkling of Hawaiian pink sea salt or tropical sea salt, if you like.

Two 14½-ounce cans coconut milk
1½ cups unsweetened shredded coconut
⅔ cup sugar
½ teaspoon fine sea salt

1 Combine the coconut milk, shredded coconut, sugar, and salt in a medium-size saucepan. Bring to a boil over medium-high heat, stirring frequently to dissolve the sugar completely.

2 Remove the mixture from the heat, let cool to room temperature, and then refrigerate for at least 2 hours or overnight.

3 Pour the mixture into the bowl of your ice cream maker and process according to the manufacturer's instructions. Transfer to a container and freeze for at least 1 hour to firm up before serving.

watermelon sorbet

MAKES ABOUT 1 QUART

In her delightful cookbook *Paris Sweets* (Broadway Books, 2002), Dorie Greenspan mentions how delicious fresh watermelon is when sprinkled with *fleur de sel*. I've tried it many times and—not surprisingly—think it's simple perfection. This sorbet is scarcely more complicated, and it's so refreshing in the summer. It's easy to make, too—but I think it's dinner-party elegant.

1 cup water
⅔ cup sugar
One 3-pound piece of watermelon, rind and seeds
   discarded, cut into chunks (about 5 cups chunks)
1 tablespoon fresh lemon juice
½ teaspoon *fleur de sel*

1 Prepare a simple syrup by simmering the water and sugar together in a small saucepan over low heat, stirring until the sugar dissolves. Let cool.

2 Combine the syrup with the watermelon, lemon juice, and *fleur de sel* in a blender or food processor and puree until smooth, working in batches if necessary. Transfer the mixture to a large bowl, cover, and refrigerate for at least 90 minutes and up to overnight. When chilled, pour the mixture into the bowl of your ice cream maker and process according to the manufacturer's instructions. Transfer to a container and freeze for at least 1 hour to firm up before serving.

sauces and other good stuff

salted **milk chocolate** sauce

Usually I prefer dark chocolate to milk chocolate, but there's something about this simple sauce that gets me every time. It's made with great-quality milk chocolate, some cream, and a hint of salt to highlight the complex notes in the chocolate. This couldn't be easier to make, and it's so great to top ice cream with a homemade sauce!

3 ounces milk chocolate, coarsely chopped
½ cup heavy cream
½ teaspoon fine sea salt

1 Combine the chopped chocolate and cream in a heavy medium-size saucepan over low heat. Heat gently until the cream starts to simmer and the chocolate reaches a melted consistency, about 4 minutes.

2 Remove the pan from the heat and whisk until the chocolate is completely incorporated into the cream. Whisk in the sea salt. Serve warm over ice cream (or anything else that's begging for chocolate sauce). The sauce will keep in an airtight container in the refrigerator for up to 1 week; warm it gently over low heat before serving.

nana's peanut butter sauce

MAKES ABOUT 3 CUPS

This recipe comes from my grandmother Betty Craven, whom I called Nana Banana. She was a wonderful baker who always had a jar of fresh cookies in her kitchen and made incredible pies at Thanksgiving and confections for the holidays. I learned from her that homemade always tastes better than store-bought. That's definitely true for this warm, gooey, delicious peanut butter sauce, which is heavenly over a simple bowl of ice cream, on top of a brownie sundae (oh, my), or—in honor of Nana Banana—on a banana split. The only change I made to her version was to add a hint of sea salt to enhance the salty flavor of the peanut butter. I have a card with the recipe written in her handwriting, which makes me smile every time I see it—and miss her so much at the same time.

½ cup packed light brown sugar
¼ cup light corn syrup
¼ cup (½ stick) unsalted butter
1 cup creamy peanut butter (regular, not natural)
1 cup heavy cream
3 teaspoons pure vanilla extract
¼ teaspoon fine sea salt

1 Combine the brown sugar, corn syrup, and butter in a medium-size saucepan over medium-high heat. Bring to a boil and stir until the sugar is dissolved, about 3 minutes.

2 Turn the heat down to low and whisk in the peanut butter. Add the cream, vanilla, and salt and simmer gently for 2 minutes. Serve warm. Or let cool and store in an airtight container in the refrigerator for up to 5 days; warm it gently over low heat before serving.

snappy butterscotch sauce

MAKES 2½ CUPS

Some sugar-based dessert sauces involve candy thermometers and precise timing. But this one, with a dash of salt and the aroma of vanilla, is amazing and super-easy to make (no thermometer required). The only key is watching the sauce carefully while it's boiling to make sure it doesn't boil over, because you don't want more mess to clean up—and you certainly don't want to waste any of this precious liquid. This is killer over ice cream and fresh fruit. For a truly decadent treat, pour it over chocolate cake or gingerbread.

1½ cups packed light brown sugar
1 cup heavy cream
¼ cup (½ stick) unsalted butter
1 teaspoon pure vanilla extract
1 teaspoon fine sea salt

1 Combine the sugar, cream, butter, vanilla, and salt in a medium-size saucepan. Stir over low heat until the sugar is completely dissolved and the butter is completely melted.

2 Raise the heat to medium and bring the mixture to a boil without stirring at all for about 3 minutes. Watch it carefully to make sure it doesn't boil over. Let cool for 5 to 7 minutes (or longer, just make sure it's still pourable), then stir and serve. Or let cool completely and refrigerate in an airtight container for up to 1 day; warm it gently over low heat before serving.

SWEET IDEAS!

* Drizzle the sauce on dessert plates and place cake or tart slices over it to serve at a dinner party.
* If you love almond flavor like I do, replace the vanilla extract with almond extract.
* Pour the sauce over roasted pears or stone fruits for a simple, elegant dessert.

caramel-fudge sauce

MAKES ABOUT 1 CUP

The name says it all: This sauce combines two of the world's most delicious flavors (those would be caramel and hot fudge) into one drool-worthy sauce. Try it over ice cream, if you can resist eating it straight from the jar with a spoon. This one makes a great hostess gift.

½ cup sugar
2 tablespoons water
1 tablespoon dark corn syrup
½ cup heavy cream
6 ounces bittersweet chocolate, chopped
½ teaspoon fine sea salt
1 teaspoon pure vanilla extract

1 Combine the sugar, water, and corn syrup in a small heavy saucepan. Bring to a boil over medium-high heat, swirling the pan occasionally and brushing any sugar crystals off the sides of the pan with a damp pastry brush.

2 Cook without stirring (just gently swirling) until the mixture turns amber colored and reaches 340°F on a candy thermometer. Immediately remove the pan from the heat and stir in the cream carefully—it will foam up quite a bit.

3 Add the chocolate and salt to the pan and let sit for 1 to 2 minutes to melt the chocolate. Add the vanilla and stir until everything is fully combined and the sauce is of a uniform consistency. Pour the sauce into a jar and let cool until thickened a bit before serving. Serve warm. The sauce will keep for up to 5 days in the refrigerator; warm it gently over low heat, stirring, before serving.

blackberry-caramel sauce

MAKES ABOUT 2 1/2 CUPS

Maybe there was a time when blackberry and slightly salty caramel didn't seem like the most obvious combination, but now that I am obsessed with this sauce, I can't remember it. When I make this, I have a hard time not eating it on its own with a spoon. I tell myself it's a healthy habit because blackberries are so loaded with fiber, antioxidants, and other good stuff. (BTW, they are!) This is fantastic served over ice cream and pound cake.

½ cup sugar
¼ cup plus 2 tablespoons water
1 teaspoon pure vanilla extract
1 tablespoon cornstarch
3 cups fresh blackberries
2 tablespoons brandy
½ teaspoon fine sea salt

1 Put the sugar in a medium-size heavy saucepan. Add ¼ cup of the water and the vanilla and bring to a boil over medium heat without stirring. Let the mixture cook for 8 to 10 minutes, gently swirling the pan every minute or so, until it turns a golden caramel color.

2 Meanwhile, combine the remaining 2 tablespoons water with the cornstarch and set aside.

3 When the sugar mixture has caramelized, turn the heat down to medium-low. Add the blackberries and brandy to the pan. The sugar mixture will harden somewhat; let everything cook together without stirring for about 3 minutes, until the berries give off liquid to dissolve the sugar.

4 Strain the mixture, reserving the berries in a medium-size bowl and returning the strained liquid to the pan. Bring the liquid to a boil over medium heat and whisk in the cornstarch mixture in small increments. Cook until the sauce thickens, 3 to 5 more minutes. Whisk in the salt until it dissolves. Pour the sauce over the reserved berries and mix well before serving warm.

strawberry–brown sugar sauce

MAKES ABOUT 1½ CUPS

A simple strawberry sauce is all you need to take a bowl of ice cream to guest-worthy status. This version is sweet but not cloying. Making it with brown sugar instead of granulated sugar and adding a hint of *fleur de sel* at the end gives it a deeper, mouthwatering flavor. Spoon some over Almond Ice Cream (page 119), Butterscotch Ice Cream (page 120), or Bittersweet Chocolate Ice Cream (page 117), or over a slice of Lemon Cake with Lemon–Brown Sugar Glaze (page 82).

2 cups hulled and halved fresh strawberries
¼ cup packed light brown sugar
1 teaspoon fresh lemon juice
¼ teaspoon *fleur de sel*

1 Combine the strawberries, brown sugar, and lemon juice in a medium-size heavy saucepan over medium heat. Stir until the sugar is dissolved, then bring to a boil, stirring and mashing the strawberries somewhat with a spoon.

2 Turn the heat down to low and let simmer for 5 minutes. Remove from the heat and stir in the *fleur de sel*. Serve warm, at room temperature, or cold. The sauce will keep in an airtight container in the refrigerator for up to 2 days.

> **SWEET IDEA!**
> Replace the strawberries with blueberries or raspberries, or try a mix of summer berries.

cinnamon-sugar sauce

MAKES ABOUT 1 CUP

One of the first salty-sweet combinations I ever remember having was cinnamon-sugar toast at my grandmother's house. She spread lightly salted butter on toasted bread right out of the oven, then sprinkled a mixture of cinnamon and sugar on top of that, which partially dissolved in the warm, gooey butter. Perhaps it wasn't a culinary innovation, but it was a delicious way to start the day. This sauce, which is amazing over vanilla ice cream or fruit, is also yummy drizzled on toast, waffles, or pancakes.

¾ cup sugar
2 teaspoons ground cinnamon
½ teaspoon fine sea salt
1 cup water
1 tablespoon unsalted butter

1 Put the sugar, cinnamon, and salt in a small container and shake to combine thoroughly. (You could stop right here and have a delicious, slightly salty cinnamon sugar for sprinkling on buttered toast.)

2 Combine the cinnamon-sugar mixture, water, and butter in a small saucepan and bring to a boil over high heat. Reduce the heat to medium and let boil gently, stirring occasionally, for about 10 minutes, until the sauce is dark brown and slightly thickened. Let cool for 10 minutes before serving. The sauce keeps in a covered container in the refrigerator for up to 3 days. Stir and rewarm in a small saucepan over low heat until just heated through before serving.

drunken sauce

This sauce has intense flavor and is nice and gooey. Your friends will beg you for more. (To quote one friend who tried it, "I'd suck it up with a straw.") This is the ideal (read: over-the-top good) companion for Chocolate Chip Bread Pudding (page 91), and the recipe makes enough to spoon about 2 tablespoons around and over each serving, which is enough to lend plenty of flavor. But if you don't want fights over who gets more sauce, you may want to double the recipe. You can also try this on ice cream or with just about any apple, pear, or fig dessert.

½ cup (1 stick) unsalted butter
½ cup packed dark brown sugar
¼ teaspoon fine sea salt
2 tablespoons dark rum
2 teaspoons pure vanilla extract

1 Melt the butter in a small saucepan over medium-low heat. Add the brown sugar and salt and stir until the sugar is completely dissolved and the sauce is smooth, about 5 minutes.

2 Remove the sauce from the heat and stir in the rum and vanilla. Serve immediately.

graham cracker **crunch**

MAKES ABOUT 1½ CUPS

During my first year out of college I worked until nine or ten o'clock every night as an analyst at an investment bank in Boston and lived in a tiny apartment (with an even tinier kitchen) on Beacon Hill. I didn't do much—okay, any—cooking then, and I missed it. One warm spring night I'd had enough, and I left the office early and invited a few friends over to sneak up to the roof of my apartment building. There was no deck up there, but it had fantastic views of the Charles River. I didn't have much time, but I wanted to make something, so I put together bowls of ice cream with juicy sliced strawberries and this crunchy graham-cracker topping. It was simple, but so tasty—and it was very satisfying to have turned on my oven and filled my little kitchen with the fragrance of something baking, even though the whole thing only took about 10 minutes.

8 whole graham crackers
5 tablespoons unsalted butter, melted
2 teaspoons sugar
½ teaspoon fine sea salt

1 Preheat the oven to 350°F.

2 Crush the graham crackers into large crumbs. Stir the crumbs with the melted butter, sugar, and salt, and stir to coat evenly.

3 Spread the crumbs on a baking sheet and bake until light golden brown, 4 to 5 minutes. Let cool, and use as a topping for ice cream, yogurt, or fresh fruit.

brown sugar whipped cream

MAKES ABOUT 1½ CUPS

Homemade whipped cream is so easy to make, and it's orders of magnitude better than anything from a can. You can play around with the sweetness and the flavoring to mix things up (try rum or bourbon, or just about any flavor of extract, in lieu of the Scotch).

1 cup cold heavy cream
¼ cup packed dark brown sugar
1 tablespoon Scotch
¼ teaspoon fine sea salt

Combine the cream, brown sugar, Scotch, and salt in a medium-size bowl. Using an electric hand mixer, or in the bowl of a stand mixer fitted with a whisk attachment, whip the mixture until soft peaks form. Serve immediately.

measurement equivalents

liquid conversions

U.S.	METRIC
1 tsp.	5 ml
1 tbs.	15 ml
2 tbs.	30 ml
3 tbs.	45 ml
¼ cup	60 ml
⅓ cup	75 ml
⅓ cup + 1 tbs	90 ml
⅓ cup + 2 tbs	100 ml
½ cup	120 ml
⅔ cup	150 ml
¾ cup	180 ml
¾ cup + 2 tbs	200 ml
1 cup	240 ml
1 cup + 2 tbs	275 ml
1¼ cups	300 ml
1⅓ cups	325 ml
1½ cups	350 ml
1⅔ cups	375 ml
1¾ cups	400 ml
1¾ cups + 2 tbs	450 ml
2 cups (1 pint)	475 ml
2½ cups	600 ml
3 cups	720 ml
4 cups (1 quart)	945 ml
(1,000 ml is 1 liter)	

weight conversions

U.S./U.K.	METRIC
½ oz	14 g
1 oz	28 g
1½ oz	43 g
2 oz	57 g
2½ oz	71 g
3 oz	85 g
3½ oz	100 g
4 oz	113 g
5 oz	142 g
6 oz	170 g
7 oz	200 g
8 oz	227 g
9 oz	255 g
10 oz	284 g
11 oz	312 g
12 oz	340 g
13 oz	368 g
14 oz	400 g
15 oz	425 g
1 lb	454 g

oven temperature conversions

°F	GAS MARK	°C
250	½	120
275	1	140
300	2	150
325	3	165
350	4	180
375	5	190
400	6	200
425	7	220
450	8	230
475	9	240
500	10	260
550	Broil	290

Note: All conversions are approximate.

index